The "Flying Scotsman"

THE WORLD'S MOST FAMOUS EXPRESS

1925

PUBLISHED BY THE LONDON & NORTH EASTERN RAILWAY
PRINTED IN ENGLAND BY KNAPP, DREWETT & SONS LTD.,
LONDON AND KINGSTON-ON-THAMES

Published in Great Britain in 2011 by Old House books & maps,
Midland House, West Way, Botley, Oxford OX2 0PH, United Kingdom.
44-02 23rd Street, Suite 219, Long Island City, NY 11101, USA.
Website: www.oldhousebooks.co.uk

A CIP catalogue record for this book is available from the British Library.

ISBN-13: 978 1 90840 208 0

Originally published in 1925 by The London & North Eastern Railway

Printed in China through Worldprint Ltd.

11 12 13 14 15 10 9 8 7 6 5 4 3 2 1

CONTENTS.

THE "FLYING SCOTSMAN" TRAIN AND LOCOMOTIVE. [*Topical.*

INTRODUCTORY

63 NOT OUT.

IN June, 1862, the day Scotch Express from King's Cross, which had, during the 8 or 10 years it had been running, left at 9.0, 9.15 or 9.30 a.m., became the famous "10 o'clock" of the railwayman, and the "Flying Scotsman" of the ordinary passenger. Since then some 20,000 journeys have been made, and as the departure time has been maintained practically without alteration during the 63 years which have passed, the "Flying Scotsman" has what is believed to be a world's record of "63 (years)—NOT OUT."*

A similar record could be claimed for the up "Flying Scotsman" had it not been for the fact that, after being scheduled in 1862 to leave Edinburgh at 10 a.m., the train was varied during following years to run at 10.10, 10.15, 10.20 and 10.25 a.m., though in 1876 it came back definitely and finally to 10 a.m.

Although the "10 o'clock" has for probably 50 years been known as the "Flying Scotsman" there is no record as to when or by whom it was first given that name. Officially, it has always been the "10 o'clock," and in the public time-tables its most ambitious title has been "SPECIAL SCOTCH EXPRESS."

*For the benefit of ultra-particular readers it may be admitted that this record is not quite beyond question, in that, during the latter part of the war period, the "10 o'clock" temporarily left 30 minutes earlier.

At first, indeed, it was dignified by a heading to its time-table column, "Spl. 1st Cl." (this was when it started earlier than 10 a.m.) and, later, "Spl. 1 & 2 Cl."

Presumably, the title of "Flying Scotsman" was given in days when fancy names for specially important trains, as also for many other things, were in fashion. At any rate, the name goes back a very long way, and was particularly suitable in that for many years this train was the chief, if not the only, day express by the East Coast Route, and was the fastest and therefore "Flying" Scotch Express.

More recently, too, though not in the public time-tables, the title "Flying Scotsman" has been given a degree of official sanction, further supported by the bestowal of the historic name upon the third of Mr. Gresley's famous "Pacific" locomotives, No. 1472 (now No. 4472), which attracted so much attention at the British Empire Exhibition of 1924, and is again being exhibited in the Palace of Housing and Transport at the 1925 Exhibition.

Apart from its claim to have the longest continuous record for unaltered departure time (it has, of course, been accelerated many times on its journey) of any express train in the world, the history of the "10 o'clock" is one of entrancing interest. In subsequent chapters the story of this famous train is briefly told, with due reference to its gradual speeding up, and the widening of its connections north of Edinburgh.

The evolution of its rolling-stock, " From Four-wheeler to 'Triplet' Dining Car " is told in a later chapter, while attention is given to the contrast between travel to Scotland in early days and the luxurious, convenient and comfortable conditions under which the same journeys are now made.

Special features which receive consideration include the famous 20-minute lunch interval at York, as to which the announcement used to read: " Hot Dinners Provided. 2s. 6d. Each. No Fees." Great stations, famous bridges and other notable features of the route account for further remarks. Lastly, not the least important chapters are those dealing with the evolution of the locomotives " From 'Locomotion No. 1' to 'Flying Scotsman'," " Clearing the way for the '10 o'clock'," and other matters of interest.

Many special illustrations are included, ancient and modern, queer and quaint, the whole constituting a record which it is hoped will be considered worthy of what is believed to be *The* " World's Oldest and Most Famous Express."

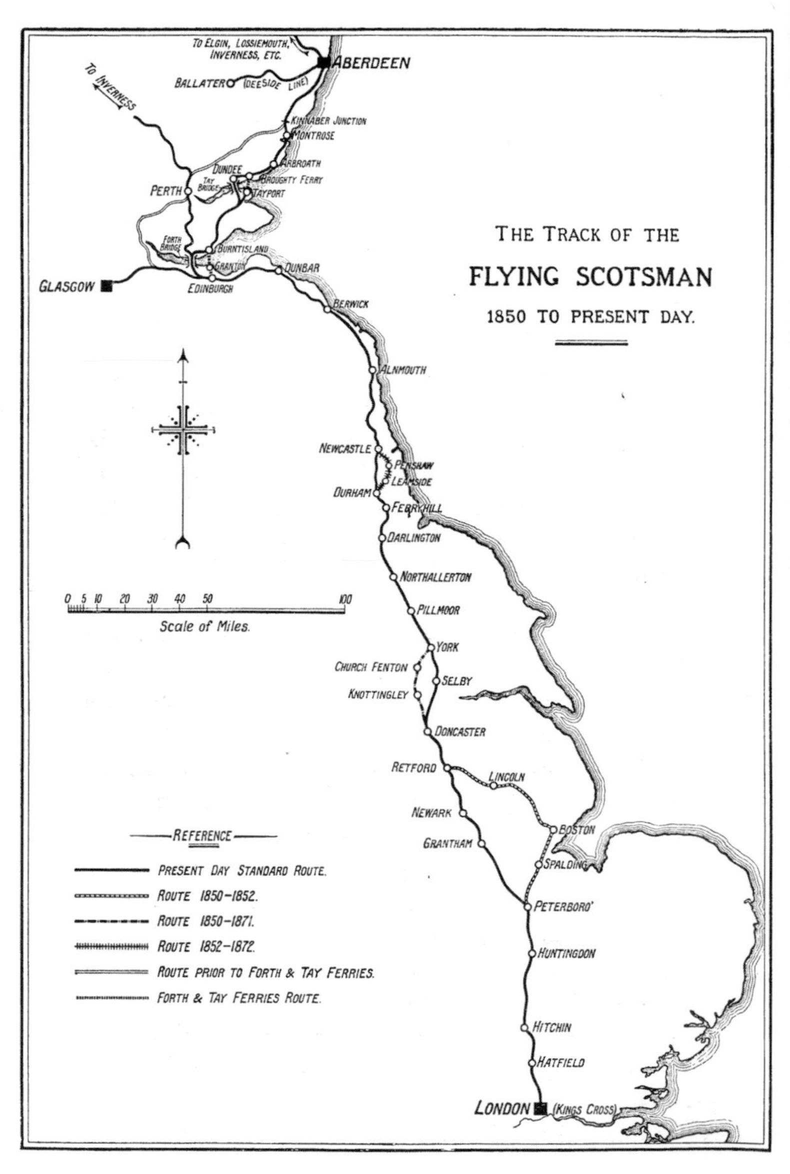
THE TRACK OF THE
FLYING SCOTSMAN
1850 TO PRESENT DAY.
TO ELGIN, LOSSIEMOUTH, INVERNESS, ETC.
ABERDEEN
BALLATER
(DEESIDE LINE)
TO INVERNESS
KINNABER JUNCTION
MONTROSE
ARBROATH
DUNDEE
TAY BRIDGE
BROUGHTY FERRY
TAYPORT
PERTH
FORTH BRIDGE
BURNTISLAND
GRANTON
DUNBAR
GLASGOW
EDINBURGH
BERWICK
ALNMOUTH
NEWCASTLE
PENSHAW
LEAMSIDE
DURHAM
FERRYHILL
DARLINGTON
NORTHALLERTON
PILLMOOR
YORK
CHURCH FENTON
SELBY
KNOTTINGLEY
DONCASTER
RETFORD
LINCOLN
NEWARK
GRANTHAM
BOSTON
SPALDING
PETERBORO'
HUNTINGDON
HITCHIN
HATFIELD
LONDON
(KINGS CROSS)
0 5 10 20 30 40 50 100
Scale of Miles.
REFERENCE
PRESENT DAY STANDARD ROUTE.
ROUTE 1850–1852.
ROUTE 1850–1871.
ROUTE 1852–1872.
ROUTE PRIOR TO FORTH & TAY FERRIES.
FORTH & TAY FERRIES ROUTE.

CHAPTER I.

BIRTH AND YOUTH OF THE "FLYING SCOTSMAN."

THE story of the "Flying Scotsman" is very nearly the history of the old Great Northern Railway, if not of the East Coast Route as a whole, so that it is necessary to start by giving a few notes as to conditions before June, 1862, when the "10 o'clock" began its long series of journeys between London and Edinburgh.

Prior to 1850, railway passengers from London to York had to travel from Euston via Rugby, Leicester, Sheffield and Normanton. But in August, 1850, the Great Northern Railway, an amalgamation of rival schemes for London and York and Direct Northern Railways, was opened from a temporary terminus at Maiden Lane (King's Cross was not then ready) to Peterborough, and, although by a somewhat roundabout route, provided a shorter and more direct journey to York without change of carriage, and more conveniently than from Euston. Trains then travelled from Peterborough via Boston and Lincoln to Doncaster, but in August, 1852, what was called the "Towns" line, via Grantham, Newark and Retford, was opened, giving a better and shorter route than via the "Loop" through Lincoln. In October of the same year King's Cross station was brought into use, so that the route as far as Doncaster was henceforth the same as it is to-day.

Between Doncaster and York, however, trains continued to travel, as they did for a number of years afterwards, over sections of what became the Lancashire & Yorkshire and North Eastern Railways, through Knottingley and Church Fenton, and it was not until January, 1871, that the direct line between Doncaster and York via Selby, was brought into use. At York, too, the situation was slightly different, in that the old station, just within the City walls, and now used as a carriage depot, was a terminal, so that trains had to reverse there.

From York to Darlington and Ferryhill the York, Newcastle & Berwick Railway provided what is practically the present-day route, but thence to Newcastle trains had to travel via Leamside and Penshaw, instead of through Durham and along the Team Valley line which dates from 1872. Approaching Newcastle the old High Level bridge was, of course, used, the King Edward VII. bridge being quite a modern one (completed 1906). The remainder of the route was substantially what it is to-day.

Apparently, through coaches were provided between King's Cross and Edinburgh almost from the first, though until 1860, when an "East Coast Joint stock" was created, the Great Northern provided all the vehicles. It is almost needless to say that they were for 1st class passengers only, for even 2nd class passengers, let alone 3rd, could not be given the privilege of through carriages all the way! Indeed, it may be questioned whether anybody not travelling First would want to go through without a break, in view of the very inferior accommodation then provided. Even 1st class passengers, for whom "Through First Class Carriages" were run "between London (King's Cross) and Edinburgh, Glasgow and Aberdeen," were not a great deal better off, at least according to modern ideas, though possibly the privilege of travelling without change of carriage for 10 to 12 hours on end was then regarded very highly!

However, in 1860 the principal day train, which had been booked to leave King's Cross at varying times from 9.0 to 9.30 a.m., commenced to convey 2nd class as well as 1st class passengers, and the "Flying Scotsman," introduced in June, 1862, did so from its introduction, and for many years afterwards. A point of special interest is that while the "10 o'clock" was in a sense an acceleration and improvement of the original train, it was actually a new one altogether for the greater part of its journey.

The time-table schedule of the first 10 a.m. indicates that it was a combination with an earlier Manchester express, the separation being made at Retford, after calling at Peterborough and Grantham. Thence the Scotch portion, passing Doncaster, ran to York, due 2.25 p.m., leaving again at 2.55 p.m. Eventually Edinburgh was reached at 8.30 p.m., that is, in 10½ hours from London, a gain of half an hour on the 11 hours of 1860.

At the same time as the down train was put on, a similar up train was arranged, leaving Edinburgh at 10 a.m., but not due in London until 9.30 p.m. Had the up train had the same unbroken record as the down " Flying Scotsman," it would also have had 63 years of continuous running to its credit. Actually, however, it changed its departure time now and then during the next few years. Thus, in 1864, it left at 10.10 a.m., with the same arrival in London, and in 1866, while the down train had been slowed a little, reaching Edinburgh at 8.45 p.m., the up " Flying Scotsman " started at 10.15 a.m. and finished at 9.35 p.m. In 1870 the down train was again booked to reach Edinburgh at 8.30 p.m.

In August, 1872, when the Great Northern Railway decided to admit 3rd class passengers to all trains, they were also allowed to use the " Flying Scotsman." Apparently, however, this caused the load to be too great for the engines of that day, so in October we find the 10 o'clock in each direction again a " Special Express 1st and 2nd Class." It was, however, much accelerated, being due in Edinburgh at 7.20 p.m., Glasgow being reached at 9.0 p.m. Third-class passengers were allowed to use the 9.0 a.m. train, which became a kind of relief to the " Flying Scotsman," as it had been continued through to Edinburgh.

Then, in the summer of 1876, came the great acceleration which made the " Flying Scotsman " a

OPENING OF KING'S CROSS STATION, OCTOBER, 1852.

SITE OF TEMPORARY TERMINUS AT MAIDEN LANE (KING'S CROSS).

ORIGINAL TICKET STATION AT HOLLOWAY.

9-hour train. This applied also to the up train, which, after having for a period started at 10.25 a.m., became again a 10 o'clock train, a time which has continued ever since. Further, while 3rd class passengers were still barred from the "Flyer," they had a reasonably good train in the 10.10 a.m. down, an improved version of the old 9.0 a.m., now running behind the main express.

So far, nothing has been said about the work of the "Flying Scotsman" north of Edinburgh, for this train has for many a year counted for a great deal more than if its usefulness came to an end when the Scottish capital was reached. As already mentioned, quite in early days the 1st Class through carriages served Glasgow and Aberdeen as well as Edinburgh. To Glasgow this was a straightforward matter, in that the old Edinburgh & Glasgow Railway provided a route from the beginning. To reach Aberdeen, however, it was necessary to make use of the rival Caledonian route, via Larbert and Stirling, and so to Perth, and over the opposition West Coast line thence to Aberdeen. To Perth this was not a very serious matter, and in quite early days fairly good services were thus available, as also in connection with the Highland Railway, for Inverness, though the route was much more roundabout than the present one over the Forth Bridge.

To Dundee and Aberdeen, however, was quite another matter, and even although through carriages were provided, the journey to Aberdeen by East Coast train must have been a painful experience, especially when the 10 a.m. from London gave an arrival at the Granite City at 3 or 4 o'clock in the morning. The situation was improved somewhat by the ferry service from Granton to Burntisland across the Firth of Forth, to join the Fifeshire lines of the North British Railway and so reach Tayport, whence another ferry connected with Broughty Ferry and thus back to Dundee or on to Aberdeen. But the Firths of Forth and Tay could both be stormy, and at times passengers who ventured by this route thought it better to defer crossing " until another day," and in any event the changing from train to steamer, steamer to train, train to steamer and steamer to train again, was not particularly attractive.

The first step was to bridge the Firth of Tay, but the original bridge came to grief after a few months' service only, and so it was not until 1887 that the East Coast Companies could announce: " From August 1st the Day Express Train service between London and Scotland by the East Coast Route will be accelerated," as a result of the opening of the new Tay Bridge, " The longest in the United Kingdom " and, of its type, in the world.

CHAPTER II.

THE "FLYING SCOTSMAN" GROWING UP.

IN November, 1887, the "Flying Scotsman" began to take 3rd as well as 1st and 2nd class passengers, though only for Edinburgh, Glasgow and the North, and not intermediately in England. It was still, however, a 9-hour train, and it was not until after the famous "Race to Edinburgh" in July and August, 1888, that any particular thought seems to have been given to acceleration. It must be remembered that the "10 o'clock" was by this time quite a heavy train, and it had to spend at least 20 minutes at York for the famous "Dinner Interval," so that the time was really quite a good one. Nevertheless, the "Race" began as a result of the announcement that the time of the 10 o'clock would be 8½ hours from July 1, 1888, and after the time had been reduced to a "best performance" of 7 hours 26¾ minutes, it was for a short period kept at 7¾ hours, and then settled at 8½ hours. Incidentally, the time of 7¾ hours has never since been repeated with this train, though for a long time it was done by one or two of the night expresses. But the day train has too much to do on the route to make such a fast time really practicable, particularly with the heavy loads always taken on the "10 o'clock," so that the real best is that which has been in force for the last 20 years or so, of 8¼ hours.

Then in 1890, after the formal opening in March, expresses commenced to use the Forth Bridge, so that the East Coast Route became not only the shortest from London to Edinburgh, but also to Perth (and therefore to Inverness), Dundee and Aberdeen, and, as a rule, has given ever since a few minutes the quicker service to all these places.

The announcement as to the new Forth Bridge services is worth quoting :—

> "From Monday, June 2, 1890, the Forth Bridge will be opened for the Through Express Trains of the East Coast Companies.
>
> "The Express Train Service of the East Coast Route will be Much Accelerated and Greatly Improved. Additional Express Trains will be run on July 1.
>
> "Through Express Trains between Edinburgh and Perth and the Highland Railway will be run via the Forth Bridge, Loch Leven and the New Glenfarg line.
>
> "Express Trains for Dundee, Arbroath, Montrose, Aberdeen, Ballater and the Great North of Scotland Railway will run via the Forth Bridge and the Tay Bridge."

The times then announced were as follows :—

King's Cross	dep.	10.0 a.m.
Edinburgh	arr.	6.30 p.m.
Glasgow	,,	7.55 p.m.
Perth	,,	8.0 p.m.
Dundee	,,	8.25 p.m.
Aberdeen	,,	10.20 p.m.

And in the opposite direction :—

Aberdeen	dep.	6.20 a.m.
Dundee	arr.	8.10 a.m.
Perth	,,	8.30 a.m.
Glasgow	,,	8.45 a.m.
Edinburgh	,,	10.0 a.m.
King's Cross	,,	6.30 p.m.

RESTAURANT CAR EXPRESS, 1880.

[" *The Locomotive* "

EAST COAST EXPRESS IN THE "NINETIES."

EARLY DINING CAR TRAIN DRAWN BY SMALL "ATLANTIC."

[" *The Locomotive* "

EARLY DINING CAR TRAIN DRAWN BY LARGE "ATLANTIC."

GROWING UP.

All this time, however, though dining cars were gradually coming into use, the "10 o'clock" kept its 20-minute "Dinner Interval" at York. Indeed, it was not until 1900 that the "Flying Scotsman" became a Restaurant Car Express, though since July 1, 1893, the new 2.30 p.m. (later 2.20 and now 1.15 p.m.) "Mid-day" Scotch Express from King's Cross had had corridor carriages and 1st and 3rd class Dining Cars. Moreover, the latter train had been provided with new and more up-to-date vehicles in 1896, so that the delay of this great improvement in the case of the "Flying Scotsman" is not easily to be understood. One reason was, undoubtedly, that the "10 o'clock" included quite a number of through coaches, to Glasgow, Perth and Aberdeen, and that it frequently required to have additional vehicles attached; its luggage and parcels business called for a great deal of van space on the various sections, and it was always a very heavy train. The "Midday" train, on the other hand, was purely a London-Edinburgh one, and considerably lighter than the 10 o'clock.

Moreover, when the "10 o'clock" at last became a Restaurant Car train, it did so in a kind of half-hearted manner at first. Thus, we find that it was only the first part down and the second part up which became "Corridor Luncheon and Dinner Trains." The first part, calling only at Newark, York and Newcastle, reduced its stay at York to 10 minutes, while the second part still depended upon the York Refreshment Rooms for Lunch, or, as it seems to have been usually termed,

"Dinner." In the opposite direction the second part had the Dining Cars.

The call of the first part down and the second part up at Newark was a rather peculiar feature, though it applied for several years. The real reason was that by running the first part through Grantham without stopping it did not block the second part which had to change engines, and Newark was then the most convenient place for changing engines on the first part. In fact, whenever the "10 o'clock" has been run in two sections, as it has for many years past for about eight months in the year, a similar arrangement has nearly always been made, though now the first part usually stops at Doncaster.

Another peculiar feature was that the two parts were both shown in the public time tables to leave King's Cross at 10 a.m. and arrive in Edinburgh at 6.30 p.m., and the same applied in the opposite direction. This was manifestly impossible, and in practice the change meant that the real time was reduced to 8 hours 20 minutes between London and Edinburgh, although on paper it still remained at 8½ hours. Actually, the second part started 10 minutes behind the first, and the first part was due at destination 10 minutes before 6.30 p.m., thus agreeing with a practice which was maintained on the East Coast Route for a very long time.

During the next few years the two parts of the "Flying Scotsman" included several variations. Thus, in 1901, the first part, though due in Edinburgh at 6.15 p.m., was not shown as an Edinburgh train at all. The explanation was that as it took only the Glasgow, Perth, Dundee and Aberdeen sections, and passengers for Edinburgh were expected to travel by the second part, there was no object in showing the Edinburgh arrival time. And, in 1906, the 10 a.m. was shown as if it ran through from London to Newcastle without a stop, the reason being that Grantham and York passengers had to use the second part. Now, however, and for many years past, the general arrangement is and has been that, whenever two trains are run, the first part (9.50 a.m.) is for Edinburgh only, calling at Doncaster, York (to change engines only) and Newcastle, while the true "Flying Scotsman" (10 o'clock) calls at Grantham, York, Newcastle and Berwick. In the opposite direction, however, the Glasgow, Perth, Aberdeen and Dundee sections, with the main Edinburgh train, are divided between the 10.0 and the 10.15 a.m. But whenever there is one train only, it, of course, includes all sections, and is then the 10 o'clock in each direction.

Finally, in concluding this chapter, it may be mentioned that in 1914 the "Flying Scotsman" was given an entirely new set of vehicles, including an all-steel kitchen car, while in October, 1924, further new trains were brought into use, including a "Triplet" Dining Car set (as described later), fitted so that all cooking is done electrically.

[*By permission of Cassell & Co.*

OPENING OF FORTH BRIDGE.

CHAPTER III.

FROM "LOCOMOTION" TO "FLYING SCOTSMAN."

ALTHOUGH even the "Flying Scotsman" express has quite a long history behind it, and can lay claim to being the oldest express train in the world so far as maintaining an unaltered departure time is concerned, one cannot help taking into account, when considering the locomotives, the famous engine which bore the number "1" on the earliest section of railway incorporated in the system over which the 63-year old "Flying Scotsman" runs. This, moreover, carries us back a full 100 years, in that it was on September 27, 1825, that George Stephenson's famous old "Locomotion" made its inaugural trip, preceded by a rider on horseback and trailing behind it a composite load consisting of coal trucks and other vehicles, some loaded with coal, but the majority with an excited crowd of enthusiastic passengers, including the band inevitable with such functions in early days.

"Locomotion" would be regarded as an erratic, clanking and cumbersome conglomeration of old iron were it not for its historic importance. Instead, however, its appearance at the British Empire Exhibition in 1924 and 1925, near by its 1922 descendant, "Pacific" locomotive No. 4472, "Flying Scotsman," accentuated the tremendous development which 100 years have produced, and the general impression conveyed was rather that of veneration for the old machine than of amusement at its queer appearance and diminutive dimensions. At Wembley the difference between the crude and elementary practice of 1825 and the advanced practice of the twentieth century was thus strongly indicated. Yet the locomotives which have successively worked the "Flying Scotsman" during its 63 years of service can trace direct genealogical descent from "Locomotion."

During the 37 years from 1825 to 1862, many and relatively rapid developments had been made, but even in the earliest days of the "Flying Scotsman" some peculiar locomotives had made their appearance on the railways which eventually formed the East Coast Route between London and Scotland.

The old Great Northern Railway, like so many of the early lines, got together, during its first ten years or so, an extraordinary mixture of engines of all shapes and sizes, but a class generally termed "Little Sharps" seems to have been the most useful. There were fifty of these engines, built by Sharp Brothers & Company, of Manchester, from which fact they were known as "Sharps" or "Sharpies." They were not exactly small—that is, for their day, though they would be regarded almost as toys now—but the builders had supplied to other railways some rather larger engines of the same class, so that it was usual to add the description "Little" to the Great Northern version.

"LOCOMOTION No. 1,"
WHICH ON 27TH SEPTEMBER, 1825, DREW THE FIRST PASSENGER TRAIN.

[" *The Locomotive* "

SINGLE-DRIVING-WHEEL ENGINES.

These little engines had a single pair of driving wheels, 5 ft. 6 in. in diameter, and weighed a mere 18½ tons. Next came some "Small Hawthorns," built by R. & W. Hawthorn, of Newcastle-on-Tyne. These were no less than 10 tons heavier than the "Little Sharps" and had 6 ft. driving wheels. They were followed by a miscellaneous lot of engines, including, in 1850, a pair of locomotives of the famous "Jenny Lind" class.

Then Mr. Archibald Sturrock came on the scene, and among the more important of his express engines were the "Large Hawthorns," single locomotives with 6 ft. 6 in. driving wheels and weighing (without tender) 27¾ tons. These engines presumably worked the "Flying Scotsman" after it became the 10 o'clock in 1862.

Mr. Sturrock then built No. 215, his famous eight-wheeled single engine, notable for its big 7 ft. 7 in. wheels. As this was built to show that it was possible to reach Edinburgh in 8 hours from King's Cross, stopping only at Grantham, York, Newcastle and Berwick (as does the "Flying Scotsman" of to-day), it is to be presumed that it sometimes worked the "Flying Scotsman" of the 'fifties, if not after 1862, as it lasted from 1853 to 1870. By 1862, however, the most up-to-date express locomotives were the 229-240 class, six-wheeled single engines with 7 ft. driving wheels, and these were almost certainly principally employed when the "Flying Scotsman" became the "10 o'clock." During the next few years, however, a number of six-wheeled four-coupled engines with 6 ft. wheels were built, as also Mr. Sturrock's 264-269 series with 7 ft. coupled wheels, with which he terminated in 1866 his period of 16 years in charge of Great Northern locomotives, and these, no doubt, were also called upon to work the " Flying Scotsman " in turn.

While, however, locomotive practice had thus developed on the Great Northern Railway, the North Eastern, which worked the Scottish trains between York and Berwick, had also seen the production of some interesting engines. These early years saw the service of a miscellaneous collection of engines, including some " Hawthorns," another famous " 215 " (a four-coupled engine built in 1853, with 6 ft. wheels), some " Jenny Linds " and others too numerous to mention, leading up to a four-coupled class completed at Gateshead Works in 1860, the " most powerful " engines possessed by the Company until 1867. These, together with another class having 6 ft. 6in. coupled wheels, no doubt took a leading share in working the " Flying Scotsman " until about 1870.

As for the North British Railway, that also had the usual mixture of engines of all shapes, sizes and classes, including those taken over from companies amalgamated with it. At that time, and until 1869, when North Eastern engines began to work through from Newcastle to Edinburgh, the North British had, indeed, the hardest part of the London-Edinburgh route, so far as gradients were concerned, so that there must have been some good engines among the locomotives possessed by them.

Returning to the Great Northern section, Mr. Patrick Stirling took charge at Doncaster in 1866, and among his earlier engines of particular interest were the first of his well-known four-coupled engines and his 7 ft. singles, the latter being probably used for trains such as the "Flying Scotsman." We have, indeed, travelled by this train even during the present century when worked by engines of the former class, old as some of them were. Before long, however, as the need for speed capabilities became more imperative—the Great Northern for a long period took the lead among British railways, and to some extent in the whole world, for speed — Mr. Stirling took the driving wheels from old No. 215 and put them into a new engine, No. 92, thus producing a larger version of his 7 ft. single-wheelers. This was in 1870, and later on he produced a large number of very similar engines, which for a long period took at least a half-share in the express work of the Great Northern Railway. We say "half-share," for in 1870 he turned out the first of his "world-famous" 8-footers, of which more models and pictures have probably been made than of any other locomotive ever built, in this or any other country.

No. 1 (illustrated on page 26) was designed in view of the increasing weight of the "Flying Scotsman" and other expresses, and was a great advance upon any engines previously built. The special feature was, of course, the 8-ft. driving wheels and outside cylinders, and the size of the engine as a whole. It was, indeed, one of the neatest and prettiest designs ever placed in service. The great point, however, was that these engines seemed able to pull phenomenal loads, as shown by the fact that they could still be seen on express trains even so recently as 1900, and fast and heavy ones at that. During both the " Race to Edinburgh " in 1888 and the " Race to Aberdeen " in 1895, they showed their speed capabilities in a remarkable degree, and more than once they covered the 105¼ miles from London to Grantham, or the 82¼ miles from Grantham to York, at over the mile-a-minute rate throughout.

Altogether there were 53 of these engines, but, alas ! only one remains, the original No. 1, preserved by the London & North Eastern Railway, because of its great historic and engineering interest. The later engines were altered a little, and the last batch, built so recently as 1895, were slightly larger, but one and all bore the chief brunt of the heavy express working between London and York until about 1900. But they had to share almost equal honours with the 7 ft. 6 in. inside cylinder singles (developed from No. 92), built by Mr. Stirling during the years from 1884 until 1892, though no representative of this class is now in existence.

Going north again, in the 'seventies the principal North Eastern express engines were Mr. Fletcher's

["*The Locomotive.*"

COUPLED ENGINES USED 1870-1890 PERIOD.

4-4-0 ENGINES, 1890-1910. [*"The Locomotive."*

four-coupled engines with 6 ft. 6 in. and 7 ft. wheels, and for many years they did most of the main line work, including the hauling of the "Flying Scotsman," well into the 'nineties, and even since 1900, though sometimes in pairs as it had become too heavy for them single-handed. Quite a number are, in fact, still to be seen on the branches. Mr. McDonnell then built a few engines, but he did not stop very long, and principal interest attaches to the so-called "Tennant" Class, Nos. 1463-1506. They were built in 1885, when Mr. Henry Tennant was General Manager and there was, for a time, no Locomotive Superintendent ; hence their name. Very similar to the later "Fletcher" engines of the 7 ft. class, they had the honour of first working non-stop trains between Newcastle and Edinburgh (1885). One of them, No. 1475, gave one of the best runs between York and Newcastle in the 1888 "Race to Edinburgh."

Meanwhile, on the North British Railway, first Mr. Drummond and then Mr. Holmes had been providing some very efficient four-coupled bogie engines with 6 ft. 6 in. and 7 ft. coupled wheels, and these worked the "Flying Scotsman" and other Scottish expresses beyond Edinburgh. During the 1895 "Race to Aberdeen," some of them took their full share in maintaining the credit of the East Coast Route. From 1898 to 1904, too, they worked some of the Scottish expresses between Berwick and Edinburgh, the opinion being held, not unnaturally, that the North British Railway was entitled to work the trains over its own lines. An attempt was, indeed, made to insist that this should apply to all trains, and as the North British officers accepted the responsibility of working the trains to time, even if it involved an additional stop to change engines at Berwick, some wonderful speed performances were done. There were runs at practically the mile-a-minute rate between Edinburgh and Berwick, and the notability of such achievements is not diminished by the fact that two engines were nearly always employed, when it is remembered that the fearsome Cockburnspath and the difficult Grants House banks had to be climbed.

In 1895 Mr. Stirling died and Mr. H. A. Ivatt took charge at Doncaster. At first Mr. Ivatt built four-coupled engines of the 400 class, but in 1898, mainly for working the Scottish expresses, he broke entirely new ground by constructing No. 990, the first "Atlantic" for a British railway. This had a leading bogie, four coupled wheels and a pair of trailing wheels. He did not build any more, however, for a year or two, as he added to his 400 class by a larger version, and constructed six bogie single engines of the 267 class. The latter did some very fine work, but the "Flying Scotsman" of 1900 was really too much for them, and it is not surprising that they were the last "single driver" engines to be introduced for working East Coast trains, and that not one of them now survives. Instead, we find, in 1900, some more "Atlantics," and these did practically all the really heavy work until they had to give place to an even larger version, of which No. 251, built in 1902, became almost as famous in its way as were the Stirling 8-footers thirty years previously. Indeed, for the next 20 years, the Great Northern was essentially an "Atlantic" line, so far as the expresses were concerned.

During these years the North Eastern Railway had been passing through a period of "compounds" (two-cylinder), under Mr. T. W. Worsdell, who reigned at Gateshead from 1885 until 1890. He was responsible for many four-coupled bogie engines, some of which took part in the 1888 "Race to Edinburgh." Incidentally, he also inaugurated the American type of cab and other features so long characteristic of North Eastern locomotives. Some of his engines shared with "Fletchers" and "Tennants" the honours of the 1888 "Race to Edinburgh," while later classes, particularly the "1630" series, did most of the North Eastern work entailed by the 1895 "Race to Aberdeen." These were the largest of the four-coupled compounds, though they did even better work when converted to non-compounds. There were also some "single-driver" two-cylinder compounds, the smaller ones with 7 ft. wheels and the larger series with 7 ft. 7 in. wheels. These also took a big share in the express working of the 'nineties, until they were superseded by four-coupled bogie locomotives.

It was in 1900, however, that the great change took place. Then Mr. Wilson Worsdell, who had succeeded his brother, brought out two new designs, one (No. 2011) of the four-coupled bogie type (the well-known Class R), and the other a six-coupled bogie locomotive (No.

2001). The last-mentioned was the first six-coupled express locomotive class in Great Britain, so that while Mr. Ivatt was responsible for the original introduction of " Atlantic " locomotives, not only on the East Coast Route, but in the whole of the British Isles, Mr. Wilson Worsdell similarly started the era of six-coupled express locomotives. No. 2001 had 6 ft. wheels only, but proved capable of doing all the speed then required on the North Eastern line.

Both No. 2011 and 2001 were subsequently developed, the former into the R 1 (1236) class, with a bigger boiler, and the latter into the S 1 (2111) class, with larger coupled wheels. Between them, these four classes for some time did all the hardest work of the East Coast Route on the North Eastern section, but in 1903 Mr. Worsdell followed Mr. Ivatt's lead and produced a North Eastern " Atlantic " design of great size and power. In the hands of Sir Vincent Raven this design was still further developed, until practically all main line work on the North Eastern line was operated by large " Atlantic " engines of a three-cylinder design, and these still take a very large share of the hardest duties.

It will thus be seen that both the Great Northern and the North Eastern lines had gradually developed into " Atlantic " lines, and as the same thing had occurred also on the North British, the whole of the East Coast Route was peculiar because of the fact that, throughout its length, from London to Aberdeen, trains

[" *The Locomotive.*"

"ATLANTIC" TYPE (4-4-2) ENGINES.

"FLYING SCOTSMAN"

"CITY OF YORK"

"WILLIAM WHITELAW"

"PACIFIC" TYPE LOCOMOTIVES.

such as the "Flying Scotsman" might be, and usually were, worked by engines of this favourite type. All of the North British locomotives were named, a practice always exceptional on the Great Northern and North Eastern lines. Mr. Reid's well-known four-coupled bogie engines of the "Scott" class have also done a great deal of heavy express work, together with his smaller-wheeled "Glens," though between Edinburgh and Aberdeen the "Atlantics" are practically always employed for trains such as the "Flying Scotsman."

This brings us to the eve of the amalgamation of the Great Northern, North Eastern and North British Railways (with others) to form the London & North Eastern Railway. In 1922 Mr. Gresley, who had succeeded Mr. Ivatt on the Great Northern, built his first "Pacific" locomotive, No. 1470, appropriately named "Great Northern." About the same time, shortly before his retirement, Sir Vincent Raven turned out No. 2400, "City of York," for the North Eastern, also a "Pacific" and, like the Great Northern engine, with three cylinders, but differing in various respects.

Then in 1923, when Mr. Gresley became Chief Mechanical Engineer of the new London & North Eastern Railway, while more North Eastern "Pacifics" were built, it was the Great Northern type which was principally multiplied. Among them was No. 1472 (now 4472) named "Flying Scotsman," and one of the principal attractions at the British Empire Exhibition at Wembley in 1924 and 1925. As, however, these engines, as built, could not run over the North British line, further engines, of which No. 2563 " William Whitelaw " (named in honour of the Chairman of the London & North Eastern Railway Company) is one, were constructed with shorter chimneys and other necessary alterations to enable them to be used anywhere on the East Coast Route.

Consequently, it is now possible, and is frequently the case, for heavy trains such as the " Flying Scotsman " to be worked by " Pacifics " of one class or another all the way between London and Edinburgh, if not on to Dundee and Aberdeen also. There are also in use some four-coupled bogie engines of what is known as the " Director " class, and these may be used between Edinburgh and Glasgow or Perth, if not elsewhere. It is, however, the " Pacifics " which now rank as the highest development of locomotive practice on the East Coast Route, and as Mr. Gresley's design is in the majority, we may conclude this chapter by inviting comparison between the " Little Sharps," " Hawthorns " and other engines of early days, and the " Flying Scotsman," which is now the " Pride of the East Coast Route."

CHAPTER IV.

ROLLING STOCK FOR THE "FLYING SCOTSMAN"

FROM ANCIENT FOUR-WHEELER TO 'TRIPLET' DINING CAR.

ACCORDING to Mr. Grinling, in his well-known "History of the Great Northern Railway," the passenger stock (for use when the first section was opened for traffic in 1848 and some years before there could be an East Coast Route or "Flying Scotsman" of any kind) which was built for the Company by Mr. Williams, of Goswell Road, at once attracted attention for the excellence of the third-class accommodation, this being described as "equal to second-class on most lines." This does not, however, interest us very much, at least at present, as it was not until many a year later that third-class passengers were admitted to the "Flying Scotsman," but we are further told that "the 'seconds,' also, were thought noteworthy for having 'good glass windows and cushions on the seat,' and the first-class were described as 'as handsome and convenient as any man of the nicest taste or appreciation of comfort in travelling could wish'." Apparently, therefore, even at that time, the Great Northern gave a lead in regard to passenger accommodation, as it did in later years on several occasions, and this is supported by a remark that, in 1858, excursion passengers were given " 15-inch seats, stuffed cushions and backs to lean against."

All the very early coaches were, of course, four wheelers, those built by Mr. Williams running on four iron spoked wheels, and weighing about $4\frac{3}{4}$ tons, less than half that of the smallest and oldest four-wheelers to be found here and there even now. But though the early Great Northern four-wheeled "thirds" were said to have been equal to or better than other railways' " seconds," they were still very crude. Apparently, they were only better than other " thirds " in being weatherproof and closed in, for they were " devoid of partitions inside, and were fitted with wooden seats ; many of them had no quarterlights, the only windows being in the doors, and at night one oil lamp in the roof supplied light for the whole carriage."

These were, of course, third class, but the second class vehicles were not a great deal better, except that they were in compartments and had, perhaps, a piece of carpet to ease the hardness of the solid seats. First-class carriages were more or less of stage-coach type, and possibly travel in them was not quite so uncomfortable as we imagine. It has to be remembered that there was a general idea that only first-class passengers would wish, or could afford, to make long journeys, and it was really a generous concession to take even second-class passengers by good trains. As for the third-class—well ! it was a pity they could

EARLY MAIN LINE CARRIAGES.

FIRST-CLASS DINING CAR.

THIRD-CLASS DINING CAR.

not or would not pay second-class fares, but that was their look-out. There was the Parliamentary all-station all-day train for them, and they must put up with the inconvenience of hard seats, draughty carriages, dim lighting, and a general jolt-up.

In 1853 the Great Northern built some of its own vehicles. The "firsts" and first and second-class composites were divided into three compartments, each having its own oil lamp. Rails were provided in the flat roof where luggage was placed, and some of them probably had the old-fashioned seats for the guard at one or both ends. In the 'sixties, that is, when the "Flying Scotsman" proper first began to run, main line coaches ran on six wheels, and in 1866 the Great Northern adopted the curved roof which remained characteristic of all its vehicles even until modern days. The early six-wheelers had four compartments first-class and five second and third, and even the main line thirds in 1866 had upholstered seats, though inferior to the seconds, and, of course, a long way behind the firsts. Those early coaches weighed about 14 tons, so that they were fairly substantially built, and compared on favourable terms with vehicles in service on other lines.

On the North Eastern Railway progress was very similar, but as, until 1861, the Great Northern provided the through coaches for the East Coast trains, we are, for the moment, principally interested in them. The first East Coast Joint Stock vehicles, too, were of Great

Northern type and chiefly built at Doncaster. The original joint stock consisted, in 1861, of 50 vehicles, in 1865 there were 63, and in 1873 they numbered 89. It may be mentioned that, as from 1st October, 1868, railways were required to provide smoking compartments for each class on every passenger train containing more carriages than one of each class, unless exempted by the Board of Trade. In 1873 sleeping cars were first run on the East Coast Route on the night expresses.

For a number of years the Great Northern type of six-wheeler was almost exclusively employed, not only for East Coast trains, but also for other expresses. Various improvements were, however, incorporated. Oil gas took the place of the original oil lamps; cushions began to include a little more padding; compartment walls were extended up to the roof instead of being open above about the level of passengers' necks; luggage racks were provided; and inside door handles were supplied as well as outside. Construction and springing were improved, and bearing in mind that these old six-wheelers frequently travelled for considerable distances almost as fast—sometimes quite as fast—as the trains of to-day, they must have been reasonably comfortable, even to modern ideas.

Then came the provision of lavatories, usually one or two to a vehicle, and the natural development was the side corridor to enable all compartments to have lavatory access. But it was not until the coming of the dining car that it became at all general to connect up vehicles to provide communication throughout. This was a somewhat belated development in the case of the "Flying Scotsman," as pointed out in Chapter I., in that the "dinner" interval at York was retained for some time after the "midday" "Scotsman" had become a dining car train. Consequently, even into the 'nineties, six-wheelers—usually, but not always, side corridor—were still being run on Scottish expresses, though eight-wheeled vehicles were rapidly displacing them.

In explanation of the apparent lateness of the East Coast companies in introducing corridor restaurant car trains for the Scottish services, it must be explained that the "dinner" interval at York was popular with many passengers. It is said that the soup was usually so hot that, while the experienced traveller went direct to the next course, the novice had only made a beginning when the bell rang and the "Take your seats, please" cry rang out. Further, the original dining cars—first run on London (King's Cross)-Leeds trains, not the Scottish expresses—were not connected with other vehicles, so that the service was restricted to passengers travelling in the cars, unless, as was done in some cases, one or two carriages were connected therewith.

When, however, the East Coast Route did introduce dining car trains—in 1893 on the mid-day service—they did things well, though even these consisted of first and third-class dining cars coupled together, the rest of the train being made up of ordinary six and eight-wheeled vehicles. The cars themselves were, however, quite good vehicles, running on six-wheeled bogies, and having clerestory roofs, Argand gas burners and steam heating. The cars of 1896 were, indeed, quite big vehicles, 64 ft. 6 in. long, 9 ft. wide and weighing 38 tons. Some of them were, in fact, quite elaborately decorated, much more so, in fact, than their modern successors, which are distinguished by neatness and simplicity rather than by the ornateness of earlier years.

Later vehicles were made somewhat lighter, but, from August 1, 1900, when the "Flying Scotsman" was given a new Corridor Dining Car set of vehicles, the modern type of vestibuled train became characteristic of Anglo-Scottish travel. Trains, as introduced on that date, consisted of eight vehicles running on six-wheeled bogies. The total length was 500 ft. and the weight 265 tons, seating accommodation being provided for 50 first-class and 211 third-class passengers. The restaurant portion extended over three vehicles, a part of the first-class car being taken up by the kitchen and pantry, while there was further pantry space in the second of the two third-class cars. A peculiar feature was that there was no right of way past the kitchen, so that passengers could not pass from one end of the train to the other, although the staff could do so. The restaurant cars were, of course, of the usual open type, and one of the other vehicles—a composite car—had the third-class compartments also of open type, though the first-class passengers in that car had separate compartments. The train was completed by two side-

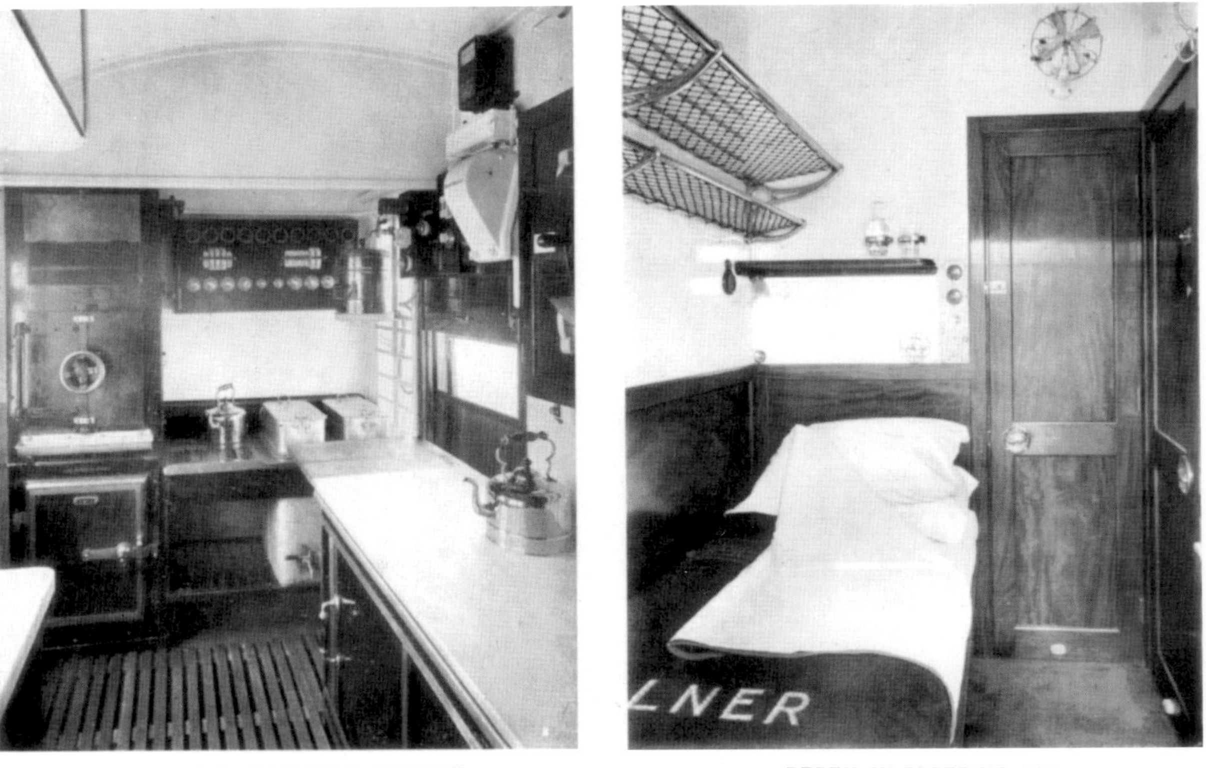

ELECTRICALLY-EQUIPPED KITCHEN.

BERTH IN SLEEPING CAR.

FIRST DINING CAR, 1879.

MODERN DINING CAR.

corridor third-class cars and by brake vans. All vehicles were vestibuled, and even at that date the couplings were of the American type still used. All vehicles had clerestory roofs, that pattern then being in fashion.

In July, 1914, entirely new stock was provided for the "Flying Scotsman," introducing a number of special features, particularly the arrangement of the kitchen in a separate car of all-steel construction in view of the fact that only there was gas used, the train otherwise being fitted throughout with electric light. The complete train was 594 ft. in length, and provided accommodation for 68 first-class and 225 third-class passengers, exclusive of the seats in the dining cars. As usual, all the new vehicles were fitted with Pullman vestibules and central "Buckeye" couplers. The first-class restaurant car provided single seats on each side of the corridor, while the third-class restaurant car had two seats on one side and one on the other. The kitchen car, which had a through corridor at one side, included a central kitchen, first and third class pantries, one at each end, and attendants' and staff accommodation. The ordinary vehicles were of compartment type, either one class only or composite. All vehicles were carried on four-wheeled steel bogies and had the now usual elliptical type of roof. They were further characterised by the improved ventilating and lighting arrangements, and the large side windows, some fitted with glass louvre ventilators and others with standard fanlights above.

A further development was made in 1924, when an entirely new type of train was provided. This consists of nine ordinary vehicles and a "triplet" dining car set, arranged according to Mr. Gresley's now well-known system, whereby three vehicles are carried on four bogies. The total length is 682 ft. and weight 370 tons. Whereas in former years, as indicated in previous references, many of the earlier restaurant car vehicles were distinguished by ornateness and elaboration of decoration, the 1924 train is characterised by neatness and simplicity in this respect. Seats in the first-class restaurant car are of armchair type. The "triplet" car set is designed so that 78 passengers can be served at the same time, although provision is made for meeting the needs of a complete train load of passengers. A special feature is, however, that the use of gas is entirely avoided, cooking and lighting being electric. The conditions under which the kitchen staff work are made much more pleasant and hygienic. Incidentally, it is recognised that food is more satisfactorily cooked by means of electric appliances than by gas. The train, as a whole, includes a large number of special features, so that the claim can be made, without exaggeration, that this represents the "last word" in restaurant car design and equipment, that is, until the time comes for the "Flying Scotsman" to be given an even more up-to-date set of vehicles.

Although the "Flying Scotsman" is a day train, there is now as much, or even more, East Coast traffic between England and Scotland by the night expresses,

TRIPLET DINING CAR SET.

TWIN SLEEPING CARS.

TRAIN SETS BUILT ON "ARTICULATED" PRINCIPLE.

so that it is necessary to add a few remarks in regard to sleeping cars. These were introduced in the late 'seventies, and if not actually responsible for providing the very first sleeping cars (other than Pullman vehicles) to be operated on British railways, the East Coast companies were at least on level terms in regard thereto. The original vehicles were, of course, relatively crude compared with their modern successors, but they were highly appreciated from the first. The modern type of vehicle with transverse sleeping compartment dates from the 'nineties, and in regard thereto the East Coast companies have always provided accommodation at least as good as, if not superior to, that provided by rival services.

In 1922 a further step was taken in providing sleeping cars of twin type, two vehicles being placed upon three bogies, the result being a combination which, in conjunction with further improvements in the equipment, gave exceptionally smooth and comfortable travelling, and more of these vehicles are being added as need arises.

CHAPTER V.

CLEARING THE WAY FOR THE "FLYING SCOTSMAN."

AT an average of one every 2 miles, there must be, between King's Cross and Edinburgh, somewhere about 200 signal boxes. Of these, probably 150 will have "home" and "starting" signals, if not an "outer home" or an "advanced starting" signal as well. The remainder may have "home" signals only, but for every box there will be at least one "distant" or repeater signal. Thus, to cover the distance of 393 miles, some 200 signalmen have exchanged bell signals and operated their block instruments, and between them have pulled off between 700 and 800 signals. Moreover, though possibly we passengers have caught only a hazy passing glimpse of, perhaps, half a dozen of these men, every one has had his eye upon us as our engine came into view, our train passed and the rear lamps faded away into the distance. Further, we might travel by the "Flying Scotsman" a dozen times and not more than once, if then, would it be necessary for our driver to sound an enquiring whistle or to apply his brakes because of an adverse "distant," while an actual stop would mean that we were being well looked after, and that we were being checked because " safety first " rendered that imperative.

Things were not always so, for even in 1862 the block system was only partially in use, while continuous brakes did not come until some years later. There were, however, fewer trains on the line in those days, and they were much lighter than they are now, while signalmen and drivers naturally did all they could to safeguard the passage of expresses such as the " Flying Scotsman " and to give them a clear path—for their own sakes as well as on behalf of the passengers. It is, indeed, remarkable, not that accidents happened occasionally in early days, but that they were so infrequent.

Further, as befitted any self-respecting railway, the Great Northern and its East Coast partners learnt from their experience, and several innovations can be traced to accidents and attempts to prevent any possibility of recurrence. Thus, the Great Northern type of " somersault " signal was introduced after the Abbotts Ripton accident of 1866. A signal became overweighted with ice and snow and showed " clear," when it ought to have indicated " danger." By pivoting the signal arm midway, instead of at one end, it was ensured that, should ice and snow accumulate, it would balance on each side of the fulcrum. It is true that there are other ways of overcoming this trouble, and only a few lines adopted the Great Northern method. But the " somersault " signal, as it is called, has remained characteristic of Great Northern signalling to this day.

Leaving King's Cross we are safeguarded by the action of the signalmen in the station box, and before our signal is lowered we may be sure that, although we are going into a dark tunnel, the road is clear for us at least as far as Copenhagen box. There we have other signals giving us the right of way to Holloway, and so, although we have to traverse a complicated and busy area all the way to New Barnet, we get signal after signal in our favour. And before any one of these signalmen, or their colleagues down the line, has pulled off the signals for us, he has sent his " call attention " and " is line clear for express passenger train " bell signals to his comrade in the box ahead, and only when the latter has sent his " acknowledgment " and " line clear " signals does he lower his semaphore which conveys so clear a warning to our watchful driver. To complete his work each signalman has sent on the " train entering section " rings to the box ahead, and returned " train out of section " to the box behind. It is true that on busy sections such as these, and at all complicated places along our entire route, the signalmen are assisted by " lock-and-block " or track circuit, so that even should one of them make a mistake and endeavour to give us a " line clear " signal in the face of danger, he could not do so. At junctions and level crossings (such as those at Retford), too, there is special locking apparatus in the signal cabins as a further safeguard. Still, however, whether they have protective assistance or not, a great deal depends on the signalmen, and it is largely due to the fact that they do their everyday work so carefully and thoroughly, and to the signal staff for designing, equipping and maintaining the signal plant, that the risk of accident on the East Coast Route, as, indeed, on any British railway, requires to be expressed as a percentage calling for a considerable number of noughts *after* the decimal point.

One other phase of our subject must be mentioned, and that is the " distant " signal, a puzzle to many people, but to the driver a most important " running " signal. This has a fishtail cut out at the outer end, and sometimes at night an illuminated fishtail shows alongside the red or green light. On the Great Northern section, however, " distant " arms are now painted yellow, and the light shows orange or green instead of red or green. Whatever the arrangement, the purpose of a " distant " signal is to give a driver warning before he reaches it that a " stop " signal is against him. Thus, if he sees a " distant " which is not clear, a driver will at once take steps to reduce speed or get his train under control, as it has told him that while he is not required to stop at this particular signal, the road is not at the moment clear for him at the next box ahead. It does not always follow that he will have to stop, as the line may be cleared for him before he arrives at the next block box, but he has been told to proceed with caution and this he does until he gets clear signals again.

Seeing that a train travelling at 60 miles an hour takes 60 seconds only to cover a mile, while a weight of,

INTERIOR OF KING'S CROSS SIGNAL BOX. [*Topical.*

SIGNALS AT WOOD GREEN.

SIGNALS AT DONCASTER. [*Topical.*

CLEARING THE WAY FOR THE "FLYING SCOTSMAN."

SIGNALS AT YORK.

SIGNALS AT NEWCASTLE. [*Topical.*

CLEARING THE WAY FOR THE "FLYING SCOTSMAN"

say, 400 or 500 tons moving at such a speed takes some stopping, particularly if travelling downhill, it is easy to understand that, if he had to wait until he saw the actual "stop" signal, a driver would not have much distance in which to pull up. Hence, the importance of the "distant" signal, one of which precedes every "stop" signal (or each series where there are several following one another, as at stations). In practice, therefore, a driver can generally assume that, so long as he has all "distant" signals clear for him, he can go ahead at whatever speed is safe. But the moment he sights a "distant" signal against him, he is all on the alert to slacken speed as required and to stop in good time when he reaches the "stop" signal of which the "distant" has given him warning.

While travelling through the complicated area, we have passed ever so many groups of signals, but as we are travelling on the through line, only the highest of those for our direction have concerned us, the others relating to local and goods lines, branches, &c. After passing New Barnet, however, we find our four lines reducing to two, and although there are many places where there are four again, a good part of our route is, henceforward, two-track only. Near all principal stations, however, and sometimes for several miles on either side, separate lines are usually provided for goods and mineral trains, and approaching places like Peterborough, Doncaster, York, Newcastle and Edinburgh, as well as elsewhere, it is usually possible for trains to travel in the same direction without interfering with us. In any event, we can usually be certain that other trains will have to wait to give us a prior right of way, or that if we are checked or stopped it is because safety requires even the "Flying Scotsman" to be pulled up.

At all big stations special protective measures are taken, so that it is practically impossible for us to be given a clear signal and another train allowed to cross or foul our path. Through tunnels, too, we are too well looked after to allow for any misgivings, though we may forgive a few nervous passengers who wish that hills and high ground did not enforce an occasional burrow underground for a quarter or half a mile or so.

Approaching the big stations we are further protected by the vigilance and knowledge of our driver and fireman. Thus, while we may rush through Hatfield or Hitchin at full speed with nothing more than a warning whistle, at Peterborough we shall find our speed carefully reduced for the severe curves there. Again, neither at Grantham, Newark, Retford or Doncaster is there need for more than careful running, but approaching York our enginemen will be "all eyes" for signals, and, with brakes carefully applied, will be ready to stop at any point of the long platform, according to length of train and the instructions of the station staff. Darlington, again, means a slight reduction of speed, and Durham a considerable one for curves and the crossing of the great viaduct. Approaching Newcastle, too, the journey over the King

Edward VII. bridge is made slowly, and there is a repetition of the York carefulness in stopping at the long curved platforms of the Central station.

Further north there are slacks for curves at Morpeth and Alnmouth; we cross the Royal Border Bridge at Berwick quite slowly, and at the station we pull up with extreme carefulness. And as we approach the complications of the Edinburgh area, once again our driver gets his train carefully in hand until he finds everything clear for him through Calton Hill tunnels and along the platform at Waverley station. Further on, too, the Forth Bridge is traversed only at moderate speed, the curves and gradients thence to Thornton Junction are taken carefully and the Tay Bridge is crossed at a medium rate, until we pull up at Dundee (Tay Bridge) station. Similarly, at other points beyond, and although we may traverse the single line sections from Lunan Bay to Hillside at full speed, we do so with the sure knowledge that our driver has possession of the electric train tablet which alone gives him authority to be on this section of line, and that, owing to the trustworthiness of the electric train tablet instruments, no other train can possibly have the same right at the same time.

Thus, from start to finish, throughout our 8¼ hours from King's Cross to Edinburgh, or our 12 hours to Aberdeen, we have had watchful eyes and capable hands exercising experienced alertness on our behalf, hundreds of other men have seen that the track is strong and safe for us, further scores have been concerned in ensuring that engines and vehicles are in the best of condition, and our drivers and firemen, not to mention guards and others, have been on the continual lookout for anything even suggestive of danger and ready to meet any emergency with trained intelligence and skill.

Yet, acknowledging all this, and much more, it is still a standing marvel that, day in and day out, for all these years, the "Flying Scotsman," together with expresses of all kinds, Scottish and otherwise, is, as a rule, given an absolutely clear road throughout its long journey, and that only in the interests of safety is it ever given an adverse signal, while an actual unscheduled stop is altogether exceptional.

Chapter VI.

A TRIP ON THE "FLYING SCOTSMAN"

London to York.

AS we are travelling in style, we arrive at King's Cross by taxi-cab, entering by the main arrival road, at the corner of Euston and Pancras Roads. After passing the "Great Northern," King's Cross Station, Hotel, well known to business men and used largely by tourists and visitors to London, our cab draws up outside the booking office, and immediately one of the porters in attendance helps us with our luggage. As there are several of us, a compartment has already been reserved, and when, with the assistance of our porter, we have located it in the Aberdeen portion of the train—we are going right through to the Granite City—we distribute our bags and umbrellas, &c., on the racks, while "father" gives a general eye to the labelling of our heavy luggage which is to go in the van.

To reserve a whole compartment costs only Five Shillings, and if there are four (1st class) or six (3rd class) passengers travelling together it is well worth the few shillings required. Otherwise, one can reserve as many seats as are required beforehand at 1s. each. Either is a great convenience, and saves any trouble in looking for seats, while the staff of the Enquiry Office on No. 10 Platform do all they can to reserve just the seats you want. Obviously, everyone cannot have a corner seat, so that, as in other matters, the "early booker secures the seat."

However, as we are in plenty of time, as soon as all this business is settled—and it does not occupy many minutes—we get out to have a look round the station. As we arrived from Gray's Inn Road we had a good view of its exterior. When put up, says Mr. Grinling's "History of the Great Northern Railway," it was "much admired," its outside was described as having "a magnificent appearance," and its inside as "presenting a vista of extraordinary effect." Indeed, some of the shareholders complained to the directors of their "extravagance in erecting so splendid a station," only to be met with the reply from Mr. Denison, the then chairman, that "it is the cheapest building for what it contains and will contain that can be pointed out in London." As the Company spent £65,000 to obtain possession of the "two old buildings that stood here" (one a smallpox and fever hospital) this went far towards the £125,000 or so credited as the cost of the station, though, so far as can be gathered, it actually involved considerably more expenditure.

The great feature at King's Cross was the inside roof, in two spans as to-day, but with one platform only under each, the present No. 10 for departures and No. 1 for arrivals. Between were fourteen carriage lines, connected crosswise by old-fashioned turntables, so that shunting, with the aid of horses or man power (the early four-wheeled coaches were not much bigger than present-day goods wagons), was much simpler than it is now.

The roof was, in its time, the largest of its kind in the world, and is said to have been modelled upon a riding school in Moscow. The girders were of timber, built up of planks bent to a bow shape. As a result, there was a tendency to spring the walls. They had sufficient support on the departure side from the range of offices and balanced on the middle wall, but along York Road there was nothing to assist and no space to provide further support. So in 1869-70, all the wooden girders of the arrival span were replaced by iron ones, a costly and awkward proceeding, while in 1886-7 the departure span was similarly dealt with.

With 10 main line trains daily (and, of course, no suburban traffic) one platform on each side was ample, and it was not until some years later that a centre platform (now Nos. 5 and 6) was constructed around the middle wall and a new platform (No. 11) provided outside the roof span on the departure side. The suburban platforms, together with the connection with the Metropolitan Railway, opened in 1866, followed at various dates.

It is now 9.50 a.m., so we had better get back to our train, but before doing so we may note the subways by which passengers are able to pass under cover, and without any need for crossing the busy roads outside, directly from the Metropolitan ("Inner Circle"), "Piccadilly," and "City & South London" stations; also the four routes for electric tramways and six for motor omnibuses which converge upon the station. Thus King's Cross is one of the most convenient of the great London termini, easily and comfortably accessible from every direction.

A hurried walk forward to see what engine we have on—one of Mr. Gresley's now famous "Pacifics," as we had hoped—and then we take our seats and settle down for a whole day in the train, yet almost, if not quite, as comfortable as if we were staying in a good hotel, if not at home. We have already noted the make-up of the train, which is as follows:—

	Length over Bodies.			Weight.	
	Feet.	Ins.		Tons.	Cwts.
Third brake	58	6	body	27	10
Luggage brake van ...	56	6	frame	26	10
Compo	61	6	,,	34	10
Compo	61	6	,,	34	10
Third	61	6	,,	34	5
"Triplet" set	153	7	body	83	0
Compo	61	6	frame	34	10
Compo	61	6	,,	34	10
Third	61	6	,,	34	5
Luggage brake van ...	56	6	,,	26	10
Totals ...	694	1		370	0

The total length of the train, over buffers is 696 ft. 1 in., the total load being 370 tons empty, and, about 400 tons full—nothing excessive, and an easy one for our big engine, but still four or five times as much as

LEAVING KING'S CROSS. [*H. G. Tidey.*

NEAR HADLEY WOOD. [*F. R. Hebron.*

ON LANGLEY WATER TROUGHS.

THE "FLYING SCOTSMAN," EN ROUTE.

the load of the "Flying Scotsman" of 1862, which probably consisted of about six passenger carriages, with two or three luggage vans, possibly six-wheeled vehicles, but more likely some of them four-wheelers only.

Punctually on the stroke of 10 o'clock we start away, without any fuss and quite easily, though our engine is not given any help from behind, as is done at some stations. As we leave the platform we note on the left the old and new suburban platforms, and the line up from the Metropolitan Railway on a gradient (1 in 43) the severity of which is obvious to the eye. We also give a glance towards the new engine sidings and the 70-ft. turntable recently provided to enable the big "Pacifics" to be turned. But it is only a glance, for almost immediately we plunge into the centre "Gasworks Tunnel" (529 yards in length). This was the original tunnel, though there are now two others, one on each side. They take their name from the now derelict gasworks which can be seen on the left-hand side.

Climbing the gradient of 1 in 105, we emerge into the open for a short distance, passing the connections with the King's Cross goods depôt and engine sheds, and under the old North London line. It was about here that the original Maiden Lane station was provided in 1850, as a temporary terminus before King's Cross was finished. Another tunnel—Copenhagen (594 yards)—and we are nearly at the top of the first steep climb. A little further on is where Holloway station used to be, but the surroundings are very different from what they were when a platform was erected there in 1854 for the collection of tickets on up trains. In those days Holloway was on the verge of the open country, while at Finsbury Park, now a busy interchange suburban junction with apparently endless sidings, the station, then called Seven Sisters Road, was merely a rough wooden platform, erected in 1861, "for the accommodation of the few residents in that rural neighbourhood" and served by seven or eight trains each way daily. The station became Finsbury Park in 1869, when the adjoining park of that name was opened.

By this time we are beginning to "get a move on," though the hard work is not finished, even for a time, by a long way. Through Harringay, past Hornsey and Wood Green (a glimpse of Alexandra Palace on the left), we are still in the midst of "bricks and mortar," but after running through Wood Green tunnel (705 yards) and passing New Southgate, signs of the country begin to show themselves. It is not, however, until we have passed New Barnet, the ordinary suburban terminus, and reached Potters Bar that we can really say we have left suburban London.

Potters Bar is the finish of our first climb, 12¾ miles calling for really "hard graft" on the part of the engine, and if we have taken only 17 or 18 minutes we have done quite well. Over the summit speed quickly rises, and for the next 60 miles we shall probably keep up a steady 65-70 miles an hour. Yet so smoothly does our train run that we hardly notice the speed, and it is only by careful calculation that we can say whether the speed is 70 or 75, or even over 80, instead of a quiet amble along at 65.

While we have been climbing to Potters Bar, a Dining Car attendant has come along and booked us for lunch, at 12 o'clock, or after leaving Grantham. Meanwhile, we run steadily along past Hatfield station and Welwyn Garden City platforms, with the St. Albans, Luton and Dunstable and Hertford branches as single lines alongside us. Then over Welwyn Viaduct, 100 ft. high, from which splendid views are had on each side, and on past Knebworth, over the Langley water troughs, where we pick up some 2,000 gallons of water, and by Stevenage and through Hitchin. Still travelling finely, at about 11.15, high chimneys on both sides indicate that we are nearing Peterborough, and are passing through the district whence come the Fletton and other bricks for which Peterborough is famous.

Next we feel the brakes go on, and a few minutes later, having taken note on our right of the magnificent West Front of the Cathedral, we pass at slow speed through the platforms of Peterborough station.

For the next mile or so we are again in the midst of sidings galore, and we may note New England yard and engine sheds on the right. Soon we pass over the Werrington water troughs, where our engine picks up, without stopping, another 2,000 gallons or so of water.

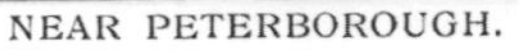

NEAR PETERBOROUGH. [*Topical.*

PASSING DONCASTER. [*B. Spencer.*

APPROACHING YORK. [*H. L. Salmon.*

THE "FLYING SCOTSMAN" EN ROUTE.

Our speed on this section, while good, and probably never below 50 miles an hour, is sufficiently slow to indicate that we are climbing again. This is the case, in fact, for about 24 miles, and it is not until we enter Stoke tunnel, the highest point of the old Great Northern line, that the gradient changes. It is of interest to note, too, that the signal box a short distance on the London side of the tunnel is exactly 100 miles from London, and that we have probably covered this in 110 minutes or less. A careful run down through Great Ponton and on go the brakes until we pull up gently in Grantham station.

Grantham is an important town, though not a very large one, but it counts for a great deal from the railway point of view. There are branches on one side to Nottingham, to which city there are many good expresses, and on the other to Boston, Lincoln, &c. Here engines are frequently changed, though it is now more usual for the engine working the "Flying Scotsman" to go through to York, but for the time being we are not particularly interested, for a more important business is in progress.

We have temporarily vacated our reserved compartment and now occupy seats in the Dining Car, and the waiters are asking us what we will have to drink (there is a wide selection, but we need not pay heavy prices unless we go in for expensive wines), or they may be already bringing along the soup. As "lunch on the train" is one of the special features of the journey—to the young mind at any rate—we are not very keen for the moment to know what engine we have on for the next stage. As a matter of fact, we have the same engine, though our London driver and fireman have been replaced by fresh men to take the train on to York.

As we get going again the fish course is served, and while our " Pacific " takes us along in good style we proceed to do justice to the well-cooked joint, the sweets and the biscuits and cheese which complete our satisfying and relatively inexpensive mid-day meal.

Between Newark and Carlton, as we cross the Trent, our engine picks up a further supply of water, and soon we are over the famous level crossing at Retford, where the old Great Central line goes right across our track nearly at right angles, and just beyond Scrooby (where we note the Scrooby Manor House, the Home of the Pilgrim Fathers), we pass over yet another set of water troughs. Shortly after Doncaster is passed where are the famous works of the old Great Northern Company, and where nearly all the engines in use on the Great Northern section of the L.N.E.R. are built, including that which, so far, has had the honour of hauling us.

Meanwhile, after coffee has been served, " father " has the privilege of paying the bill—not a very dreadful one—and we wend our way back to our reserved compartment, enabling a second relay of passengers to have lunch in their turn. Before settling down again, however, a visit to the lavatory enables us to wash our hands (hot water available if desired), and we find an ample supply of clean towels.

Still our "Pacific" keeps pegging away, rarely much below the mile-a-minute rate and usually faster. We have passed Shaftholme Junction (where the Great Northern Railway used to join the North Eastern), and on the way to Selby, where we slacken speed to cross the swing bridge there, giving the opportunity for a good view of Selby Abbey. Further on, at Chaloner Whin Junction, we are joined by four lines on the left, the original route by which the "Flying Scotsman" travelled when it ran from Doncaster via Knottingley and Church Fenton. A mile further and we pass the platforms at Holgate Bridge, the old ticket platforms for York station, but now only used when special trains are run for York races. Just beyond we catch a glimpse of lines on the right passing through an arch in the walls of York City. These lead to the original station, a terminus, but for many a year, since 1877 in fact, used only for storing and cleaning carriages. Now we run smoothly under the great roof of York station, and make our second stop at the long curved platform of No. 5, 1,575 feet long.

Besides our own platform there are 13 others, though it is difficult to realise this. Opposite us, on the right, is No. 4, the main up platform, 1,692 feet in length.

The great feature of York station is that the artistic roof, curving to follow the contour of the through

YORK STATION: No. 4 (South) PLATFORM.

platforms, gives so splendid a vista, though to appreciate this one requires to be there at a quiet period, and not when the "Flying Scotsman," up or down, is standing at a platform. There are through lines between Nos. 4 and 5, and when the 10 o'clock is preceded by its relief train at 9.50 a.m. from King's Cross, that train usually stops on the middle line to change engines, though it is not booked to call at York to take up or set down passengers.

Had there been time we might have had a look round York, for it is well worth a day or two's stay, say, at the Royal Station Hotel. Incidentally, there are few more interesting walks than that along the old City walls, from which we can look down on the original station—now shorn of its ancient glory—and give a glance over the present station or observe the towers of York Minster not far away. But our ten minutes are up, and so we rattle over the crossing at the north end of the station, on our way to our next stop at Newcastle.

CHAPTER VII.

A TRIP ON THE "FLYING SCOTSMAN"

YORK TO NEWCASTLE.

OUR engine on this stage is an "Atlantic," one of Sir Vincent Raven's well-known three-cylinder class. We might have had another "Pacific," but to-day we have one of the ordinary engines which until recently did all the heavy express work on this section.

Once clear of York station and past Clifton Junction engine sheds and sidings, we gather speed rapidly, for London & North Eastern engines are noted for getting away quickly, and we have before us a stretch of 44¼ miles to Darlington, ideally laid out for speed. It is, indeed, the "racing ground" of the old North Eastern line, and it is here, though in the opposite direction, that the up Glasgow-Leeds "Flyer" is booked to cover the 44¼ miles from Darlington to York in 43 minutes, start to stop, *i.e.*, 61.7 miles an hour.

Consequently, after leaving the Harrogate branch to the left, we have a clear run, never below 60 miles an hour, to Thirsk, passing Alne, where one may get a glimpse of the Easingwold Railway train, if it is in the station. This is the smallest railway in the British Isles —2¼ miles long, possessing one engine and three tiny carriages.

Thirsk is a busy centre, for here come in lines from Harrogate and Leeds direct, but we dash on to Northallerton and over connections with still another line from Harrogate and Leeds, and branches, one to the left up beautiful Wensleydale to Hawes Junction, and another on the right to busy Stockton and Middlesbrough. Still we continue at full speed, covering the miles in a trifle under the same number of minutes, and picking up water between Northallerton and Danby Wiske. Then on past the branch to Richmond and Swaledale and so to Croft Spa. After traversing a maze of sidings and connections, a line from Stockton and Middlesbrough by the old Stockton & Darlington Railway comes in on the right. We do not go through Darlington station, so that there is no opportunity to notice the pedestal where George Stephenson's "Locomotion No. 1" stood so long and where it will, no doubt, stand again after it has figured in the Railway Centenary celebrations of 1925. Instead, we go behind the station, on the through lines, and proceed on our way, after leaving the Barnard Castle and Teesdale branch on the left, to Ferryhill.

This is another important junction station, where trains come in from Stockton and Middlesbrough, and leave at the north end for Bishop Auckland, the Hartlepools or Leamside, and so over the original route to Newcastle avoiding Durham.

Now on the direct line to Newcastle, which was opened in 1872, we notice a change. No longer are we

LEAVING YORK. [*H. Gordon Tidey*

ON WISKE MOOR WATER TROUGHS. [*W. Rogerson.*

PASSING CROFT SPA. [*W. Rogerson.*

THE "FLYING SCOTSMAN" EN ROUTE.

HIGH-LEVEL BRIDGE. [*Central Press.*

KING EDWARD BRIDGE.

CENTRAL STATION.

NEWCASTLE-ON-TYNE.

on easy gradients, and while the country is still beautiful—very much so as a rule—frequent collieries explain why, even on the downhill stretches, we have to go carefully, for the land is honeycombed with coal workings, and here and there it may be necessary to avoid exceptional speed while, after crossing the Croxdale Viaduct, we have a hard climb up to Durham.

Before reaching that ancient city we have a fine view of Dearness Viaduct, on the Waterhouses branch, as it comes in to join us at Waterhouses Junction. The scenery here is a mixture of natural beauty and colliery rubbish heaps, but any disappointment we may have because of the latter is amply compensated for as, at reduced speed, we pass on to the great viaduct which leads to Durham station. Here one overlooks the old city, with splendid views of the Cathedral and Castle, and of the picturesque River Wear.

We are now on the "last lap" of the York-Newcastle stage, and though we may not do any specially fast running, we continue at a good speed. All along here are signs of the Durham coal industry, lines for mineral traffic parallel our own, and sidings, mostly full of coal wagons, surround us on every side as we get a general view of Newcastle and Elswick in the distance.

Near Bensham we leave the old line which continues through Gateshead and thence into Newcastle Central at the east end over the High Level bridge, while we ourselves curve away towards the King

Edward VII. bridge, opened in 1906. As we cross the bridge, at a height of 82 ft. above the river, we have a fine view of the Redheugh bridge to the left, and of the High Level bridge to the right, but, almost before we know it, we curve away to join the Newcastle and Carlisle line, and pass under the wide roof of Newcastle Central station at the west end.

This station is laid out on a curve, and presents an appearance not unlike that of York. It is, however, older than the present York station, so far as the original part is concerned, but until we leave again only a portion of it comes into view. We stop at No. 8 platform, though were it necessary we could be sent over to No. 9 or No. 10, on either side of a great island platform, for here, as at York, the through platforms can be used for either-way traffic.

Before the King Edward bridge was completed, all trains from the south had to cross the Tyne by means of the old High Level bridge, and as they left again for the north at the same end of the station it followed that the new engine had to be attached at the rear end of the train and the rest of the journey was made the other way round. Now, however, all principal trains come in over the King Edward bridge and continue northwards without reversing, and the only disappointing feature is that we do not go over the High Level bridge with its roadway below. That bridge is now used principally by South Shields and Leamside trains, together with expresses via Sunderland, the Hartlepools and Stockton. The High Level bridge, it may be mentioned, is 112 ft. high and 1,338 ft. long, in six spans. In crossing one looks down on the swing bridge (road) below, but if walking over one gladly pays the ½d. toll demanded of pedestrians, if only to avoid the steep descent to the swing bridge and the climb up on the other side.

Finally, we may notice ahead of us, as we stand in the Central station, the historic Black Gate and the Cathedral Church of St. Nicholas.

AT NEWCASTLE. [*Topical.*

NEAR BELFORD. [*C. J. L. Romanes.*

LEAVING BERWICK. [*C. J. L. Romanes.*

THE "FLYING SCOTSMAN" EN ROUTE.

Chapter VIII.

A TRIP ON THE "FLYING SCOTSMAN"

Newcastle to Edinburgh.

EIGHT minutes are allowed at Newcastle (Central) station, and the " right away " signal is given as the big clock shows 3.39 p.m. This time we have another " Pacific," but one of Sir Vincent Raven's three-cylinder class, though we might have had a Gresley engine of the same type, as fitted for running on the North British section of the L.N.E.R. However, we are well pleased, as we have thus had representatives of all the locomotive classes now usually employed on " the Flying Scotsman " south of Edinburgh.

Starting away in easy fashion, we rattle over the famous crossing at the east end of the station, leaving the High Level lines to the right, and curve away towards Manors station, continuing over the electrically fitted lines used by direct Tynemouth and Riverside electric trains for another mile or so. Passing over the Ouseburn Viaduct we note Byker Viaduct (road) on the right. At Heaton Junction we see the carriage and electric train workshops, and after passing through another maze of sidings leave the electric trains to themselves and turn northwards towards Forest Hall. For many miles yet we are accompanied by outward and visible signs of the importance of the Northumberland coal area.

In passing Killingworth a glimpse may be caught of George Stephenson's old house, and if our eyes are sharp we may be able to distinguish also the sundial over the front door, made by him.

By this time the Dining Car attendants have invited us to adjourn to the car again for tea, which we do with pleasure, returning to our compartment in good time to enjoy the views of the coast to be had from the train between Alnmouth and Berwick. Onwards past Chevington Junction (for the Amble branch), and Warkworth (a glimpse of Warkworth Castle on the coast), we continue to run smoothly over the easy or gently undulating line to Alnmouth Junction. Here diverges the branch to Alnwick and the beautiful Coldstream and Kelso line. Alnmouth is itself a seaside resort, and from this point onwards, nearly to Edinburgh, in fact, the East Coast Route is an actual East Coast line, frequently, if not always in direct view of the sea.

From Alnmouth Junction we cross a viaduct over the River Aln, and then start a four mile climb at 1 in 170 up the Longhoughton bank, which extends nearly to Little Mill station. Here we are running downhill again and speed quickly rises to about 70 miles an hour and continues at about that rate for the next 20 miles or so. On this section, as we pass Christon Bank, Chathill (for the queerly named North Sunderland

Railway to Seahouses), Newham, Lucker, over a set of watertroughs, Belford, Smeafield, Beal and Goswick, we have many views of the sea over the cliffs.

In passing we may note the coastguard station at Embleton Bay, the Farne Islands and their two lighthouses out to sea, Bamburgh Castle and Holy Island, to which there is a low-tide path marked by stakes. Beyond Goswick, there is another climb of three miles at 1 in 190 to Scremerston, followed by a run down to Tweedmouth Junction, where we note the line from Coldstream and Kelso climbing towards us on the left. Here we have a general view of the border town of Berwick-on-Tweed, neither in England nor in Scotland, and then go easily over the famous Royal Border bridge. This is 2,160 ft. long, with a maximum height of 126 ft. It was opened by Queen Victoria in 1850. There are 28 arches, and as we cross it we have magnificent views on the left of the scenic beauties of the Tweed, on the right of the ancient stone bridge built in 1634, and out to sea of Holy Island, Bamburgh Castle and the Farne Islands.

Immediately on leaving the bridge we enter Berwick station, now in process of rebuilding. Meanwhile, it calls for reduced speed if we are not to stop, but as the "Flying Scotsman" is booked to call there we pull up gently at the platform. Before long the Berwick station will rank among the best on the East Coast Route.

Starting afresh, we commence with four miles or so at a gradient of 1 in 190 against us, but the moderate

ROYAL BORDER BRIDGE, BERWICK-UPON-TWEED.

speed is more than compensated for by the many glimpses of rocky coast which reveal themselves here and there as we look down rugged ravines, or the views of bay and sea which can be had whenever the walls of the cuttings do not intervene. But we are not yet in Scotland, for it is not until we pass Lamberton Toll, about three miles north of Berwick station, that we cross the border.

At Burnmouth we have a passing glimpse of the picturesque village and harbour of that name, while a branch line runs alongside, though descending to a lower level, for about half a mile before it leaves us to reach the village of Eyemouth. Then at good speed past Ayton and we start our seven-mile climb to Grants House, beyond which, at Penmanshiel tunnel, we top the summit of the East Coast Route. From our point of view, however, to reach it has involved only a steady pull on the part of the engine, but were we travelling in the opposite direction we should have had to climb the much more difficult Cockburnspath bank, five miles at 1 in 96, double the steepness of the southern side.

We now have the bank in our favour, and so run down at good speed through Cockburnspath and on through Innerwick to Dunbar, still, however, with occasional views of the coast and the open sea, also of the ruins of Innerwick Castle, Barness Lighthouse, and the Bass Rock opposite North Berwick ahead of us.

Some express trains call at Dunbar, a favourite holiday resort and residential town, but the "Flying Scotsman" passes behind the station on the through lines without slackening speed, and continues on past East Linton and East Fortune. Near the latter we get a view of North Berwick Law, a peculiar mound overlooking the pretty residential and holiday town of North Berwick, and then, as we approach Drem Junction, the North Berwick branch come in alongside.

As the route is now relatively level, a good speed is maintained past Aberlady Junction and Longniddry Junction, while beyond this point we continue at more moderate speed, for we have reached a district where junctions and sidings are numerous. There is, however, still a good deal of the scenic element, and near Prestonpans glimpses are had across the waters of the Firth of Forth and even of the Fife coast beyond.

At Inveresk the Gifford branch and the Waverley line from Carlisle join us on the left, and at New Hailes the Musselburgh line. Then past Joppa and Portobello, both serving residential seaside districts, and so, amidst a maze of junctions and lines, we run through Calton tunnel and pull up at the main down platform of Waverley station, Edinburgh. We have run the 57½ miles from Berwick in a shade under the 72 minutes allowed, and have completed the journey of the "Flying Scotsman" proper, from London (King's Cross) to Edinburgh, in 8¼ hours for the 393 miles, including stops at Grantham, York, Newcastle and Berwick.

NEWCASTLE TO EDINBURGH.

Waverley station, the largest in Scotland and the second largest in Great Britain, is one most strangely yet interestingly situated, though this is not apparent unless we can break our journey in Edinburgh, instead of continuing as we are going to do on this occasion.

As, however, we do this on our return journey, a few remarks may be interpolated here.

The station consists of one huge island platform, probably the largest in the world, 285 ft. wide and 1,680 ft. long on each side. In the centre is a block of buildings containing the booking offices (with much fine cabinet and stone work), refreshment rooms, waiting rooms, &c., including a lift and private way direct to the adjacent North British Station Hotel. North and south of the block there are 15 terminal platforms, 7 at one end and 8 at the other. Outside each of the through line platforms (Main Up and Main Down) are tracks used for shunting and storing carriages, the whole being under one roof, which thus extends to nearly 18 acres. Outside the station proper, reached by the main footbridge, is a small island platform belonging to what is called the "Suburban" station. Consequently, there are no fewer than 19 platforms, and as each of the main platforms is long enough for two trains at once, Waverley could actually contain 21 trains simultaneously.

Ascending by the slope to Waverley Bridge and then proceeding up to Princes Street and round to the North Bridge, or climbing up the Waverley Steps

THE "FLYING SCOTSMAN' AT EDINBURGH (WAVERLEY STATION).

(" windy corner " when the wind blows, as it usually does in Edinburgh), and thence to the North Bridge another way, we have quite another aspect of Waverley station. Then we realise its remarkable situation, at the bottom of a deep gorge, with the high ground of southern Edinburgh on the left, the rocky mass upon which stands Edinburgh Castle and The Mound (with its Museum and Picture Gallery) in front, and to the right beautifully laid-out gardens sloping down from Princes Street—said to be one of the world's finest thoroughfares—with the Scott monument as the most conspicuous feature of the view. Beneath us is the great station, though virtually nothing is to be seen of it from this point, owing to the fact that it is entirely covered, except at the extreme ends. To see anything much of it from above one must go a little way along Waterloo Place, or go round into old Edinburgh via High Street for the east end, or find one's way to the lower paths of Princes Street Gardens which overlook the station at the west end, and thence to The Mound, where west-bound trains pass under in tunnel. Seen from the west, the view then includes the great mass of the North British Station Hotel, the largest and finest in Scotland, with its splendid clocktower extending to a height of 170 ft. above Princes Street, the neat span of the North bridge, to the left Calton Hill, and to the right Arthur's Seat.

It is doubtful, indeed, whether any other railway station in the world has so remarkable a location. Certainly there is not one of equivalent size and traffic importance, though the unique features cannot be fully realised unless actually seen. In any case, the tourist who fails to break his journey at Waverley station misses an opportunity which he must ever afterwards regret, for Edinburgh is a place full of historic, scenic, architectural and tourist interest, and is itself one of the finest centres for a holiday. It has the further advantage, possessed by few tourist centres, that so much of the interesting ground is handy, if not within the limits of the city itself, while quite short journeys only are required to reach scores of other places equally attractive in various ways.

CHAPTER IX.

A TRIP ON THE "FLYING SCOTSMAN"

EDINBURGH TO DUNDEE, GLASGOW AND PERTH.

BUT while we have been enthusing on the subject of Waverley station and of Edinburgh as a holiday and tourist centre, the train in which we came from London has been dismantled and its parts scattered about the station. Part of the train, including the "Triplet" dining car set, has been drawn forward, to be put away, after all luggage has been removed, until to-morrow's up "Flying Scotsman." The Glasgow coaches, behind one of the busy little shunting engines of which a number are moving about the station all day long, are taken to the platform from which starts the 6.30 p.m. Glasgow express. The Perth coaches are taken by another engine to the 6.38 p.m. train, and, finally, our Aberdeen coaches are added to the 6.32 p.m. express, already partially made up. Actually, there is no need for us to remain in our compartment. But if we leave it, it is necessary to find out the platform whence our journey will be continued, and as we shall have an opportunity of "seeing Edinburgh," and, of course, Waverley station, at convenience another day, we do as most through passengers do—ensure by remaining in it that we do not lose our carriage.

We find, on our Aberdeen train, another restaurant car than that we have used as far as Edinburgh, equally comfortable, and equipped for serving dinner of the same standard of excellence as the lunch which we had so much enjoyed on the Grantham-York stage of our journey, though of a more usual type.

Punctually at 6.32 p.m. we start away, this time headed by a large-boilered North British "Atlantic" with a Scottish name, but painted the same green as the engines we have had so far, and bearing also the now familiar initials L.N.E.R. As we are travelling while the days are at their longest, allowing for the "Summer Time" hour, which at this time of year is so much appreciated by holiday-makers, if not by farmers, we shall be able to reach our destination before darkness falls. We shall thus have the advantage of enjoying all the scenic attractions of the northern part of the route of the "Flying Scotsman." It is true that the original "Flying Scotsman" was only indirectly an Aberdeen train, for in early days the "Granite City" was served by means of connections and by a complicated and circuitous route, as explained in an early chapter. But for many a long year, since, indeed, the Forth Bridge was opened in 1890, the Aberdeen and Perth sections of the train have ranked only secondary to the Edinburgh portion in importance.

By this time we have passed between the Princes Street gardens, through the short tunnel under The Mound (124 yards), along the base of the great rock

EDINBURGH (WAVERLEY STATION). *'The " Locomotive."*

PASSING PRINCES STREET GARDENS, EDINBURGH.

ON FORTH BRIDGE. [*Special Press.*

ON TAY BRIDGE.

THE "FLYING SCOTSMAN" EN ROUTE.

on which stands Edinburgh Castle, and through Haymarket Tunnel (1,000 yards). Haymarket station is passed without calling, and, gradually accelerating, we continue, with a glance at the Haymarket engine sheds, along the old Edinburgh & Glasgow Railway as far as Saughton Junction. Soon we leave the crowd of sidings which have surrounded us from Haymarket station, and gather speed as we make for the open country and the Forth Bridge. Already the Scottish dining car attendants have booked us for "dinner," and as the calls of the "inner man" (or woman) are making themselves apparent, we take our seats in the Dining Car. While dinner is being served we are speeding through Turnhouse, and over an undulating and at times steep course to Dalmeny. Here, after noticing several low level lines below us we approach the "world's greatest railway bridge" at about 40 miles an hour, the usual speed when crossing.

Were we able to lean out of the window, which we cannot do while in the Dining Car (it is a dangerous practice in any case), we should be impressed by the view thus obtained of the Forth Bridge, as it towers above us to a height of some 150 ft., but disappointed owing to the fact that it is then seen end-on. However, this sense of disappointment soon gives place to interest as the train passes on to the bridge itself, below and between the maze of 12 ft. tubes and criss-crossing girders, and one looks out over the waters of the Firth some 150 ft. below. Inland one looks up the Firth and perchance notices an apparently toy steamer plying across or along its waters. Seawards, a view can be had right out to sea, while when about half-way across, one can look down, on the right-hand side, upon Inchgarvie island. Here still exist the foundations for the centre pier of the first, but never completed, Forth Bridge. Work had been started when the original and ill-fated Tay Bridge collapsed on that stormy night of December 28, 1879. This revealed that, along these open Scottish Firths, stormy winds could blow with a force which had not previously been realised. So work was suspended on the Forth Bridge and an entirely new design prepared, and, as a result, the great structure which has so far stood the force of wintry gales for 35 years, and is good for many more, was erected at a cost of over £3,000,000.

For about two minutes we are on the Bridge, somewhat neglecting dinner meanwhile as we attempt to look out on both sides simultaneously, and regretting that we cannot look up also to see the mighty mass of the upper works towering above us. Then we give a passing glance on the left to the harbour of North Queensferry on the Fifeshire coast. After passing North Queensferry station we see no more of the waters of the Firth of Forth, at least in the vicinity of the Forth Bridge, as we plunge between the walls of rock cuttings.

Below us a view is had of the low-level line leading to North Queensferry Harbour and Pier, and then at Inverkeithing we leave the Perth main line as it turns inland to Dunfermline. More rock cuttings, with a

FORTH BRIDGE. [*Photochrom.*

glimpse of Inverkeithing Harbour, and of Inchcolm Island out in the middle of the Firth, and we climb up a grade of 1 in 94 for a couple of miles or so to Aberdour.

Aberdour is a favourite holiday resort, as also is Burntisland, though the first view we have of the latter is of its coal sidings and manufactories. Passing the station we have a good view of the harbour and may catch a glimpse of the old station buildings which did duty when the route from Edinburgh to Dundee and Aberdeen involved crossing the Firth of Forth from Granton to Burntisland by steamer. Beyond the station we then run along the very edge of the land, overlooking a magnificent stretch of sand, which attracts so many Scottish workers, with their families, to Burntisland.

These sands extend all the way to Kinghorn, another favourite holiday resort, and after passing through Kinghorn tunnel we have, looking backward, a fine view of the bay as we curve round its shores. Then on to Kirkcaldy, a busy manufacturing town, its principal product being floorcloth. It is often spoken of as the "Lang Toun," as it is long-drawn-out for a length of about three miles.

Stopping at Thornton Junction—the station is laid out as an island, with terminal bays at each end—for a few minutes to take on Glasgow passengers, we start on our run across country to the town of Cupar, where we stop once more for a couple of minutes. Then on to Leuchars Junction, where connection is made with branches to St. Andrews, the " home of golf," and accommodating one of the principal Scottish universities, and to Tayport. Passing at Leuchars Junction the triangular connections with the Newburgh and North Fife line and St. Fort station, we come in sight of the waters of the Firth of Tay. As we do so we join the coast line from Tayport, close to Wormit station, though we do not go through it. Then on to Tay Bridge, the last of the " bridges " which earn for the East Coast the title of " Great Bridges Route."

Unlike the Forth Bridge, the Tay Bridge is only a moderate height above water level, and it is really in the nature of a viaduct—the longest (2 miles) of its kind in the world. The present bridge was opened in 1888, so that it has weathered the storms of 37 winters. It is double-track, with no fewer than 85 spans. Those in the centre are designed for the passage of shipping along the Firth. Then a sharp curve through Esplanade station, and we run down gently into Tay Bridge station. This is in the form of a big island, and there is usually a large interchange of passengers, for Dundee is one of the great manufacturing towns of Scotland, so that we stay here for several minutes while we change our Edinburgh " Atlantic " for another one of the same class.

Meanwhile, although we ourselves have travelled through with the Aberdeen section of the " Flying Scotsman," we must not forget that at Edinburgh there were two other portions, which, while we were making our

TAY BRIDGE. [J. *Valentine.*

way to Dundee, were proceeding to Glasgow and Perth respectively. One of them, indeed, left Waverley station before we did, attached to the 6.30 p.m. Glasgow express booked in the even hour. This is a hard run, though over a fairly level route—except from Cowlairs down into Queen Street, Glasgow, where the incline of two miles at 1 in 45 has to be descended so carefully that it takes nearly as long to go down as it does to climb in the opposite direction. There is nothing very special about this route so far as scenic interest is concerned, though some pretty parts are traversed, particularly in the neighbourhood of Linlithgow. But as some of the trains are quite heavy—and the 6.30 p.m. from Waverley is no exception—the engines employed have to be worked hard to keep time, whether of the North British " Scott " or the new L.N.E.R. " Director " class of 4-4-0 locomotives.

Queen Street Station, Glasgow, is well situated so far as the city is concerned, and there is another of the well-known London & North Eastern Hotels adjacent to it. Being at the foot of the Cowlairs incline it is necessary for all east-bound trains, except the lightest, to be assisted, usually by an engine behind. In the case of trains not calling at Cowlairs the banking engine is " slipped " at the summit. Possibly it will be remembered that for a great many years trains were assisted up the incline by a haulage cable worked by a winding engine at the top, and in connection with this the " first signal box in Scotland " was erected. The old winding engine, by the way, completed about 60 years' service not a great while back, when it was dismantled and scrapped.

The Perth coaches of the "Flying Scotsman" left Waverley station six minutes behind the Aberdeen portion and followed us over the Forth Bridge as far as Inverkeithing Junction. There they diverged towards Dunfermline (Lower) where they made a brief stop, thence traversing part of the Fife coal area to Kinross Junction, where connection was made with a line from Stirling. At Mawcarse Junction the branch to Ladybank Junction was passed, while the express continued on, through increasingly beautiful country and over increasingly difficult gradients, to lovely Glenfarg. Then through the Glenfarg tunnels and along the beautiful Glen from which the station takes its name to Bridge of Earn where, if there were any passengers from south of Berwick, a momentary stop was made. Another four miles or so and the line from Stirling was joined, and finally, after running through another tunnel, the train drew up at Perth General (Joint) station. As the time was 7.35 p.m. there was little likelihood of any passengers requiring to travel through to Inverness without a break, so there is no connection, but, in the case of the night East Coast expresses, not only through carriages, but sleeping cars also, not infrequently as long and heavy complete trains, work right through from London to Inverness. Certain day trains from Edinburgh, too, go right through, and some of these include restaurant cars.

Chapter X.

A TRIP ON THE "FLYING SCOTSMAN"

Dundee to Aberdeen.

STARTING again from Dundee (Tay Bridge Station) we pass into Dock Street tunnel (622 yards) and then climb up a grade of 1 in 60 in order to traverse the dock area at road level. A line has joined us from the station known as Dundee East, for as far as Arbroath the line is a jointly owned one known officially as the Dundee & Arbroath Joint Railway. A notable feature of this route is that we have the docks on the right and there are frequent footbridges and several level crossings giving access thereto. Indeed, were we passing at, say, a minute or so after 12 noon, we should find these footbridges packed with dock workers or crowds waiting at the crossings as they leave for the dinner interval.

Soon, however, we leave industrial Dundee and, gathering speed, for the next stage is a fast one, we pass through West Ferry and Broughty Ferry, both neat residential districts, while the latter was, in earlier days, important as the port for the ferry service across to Tayport which maintained communication before the Tay Bridge was available. Then on through Carnoustie (a favourite holiday resort) to Elliot Junction,

AT DUNDEE (Tay Bridge Station).

ON MONTROSE VIADUCT.

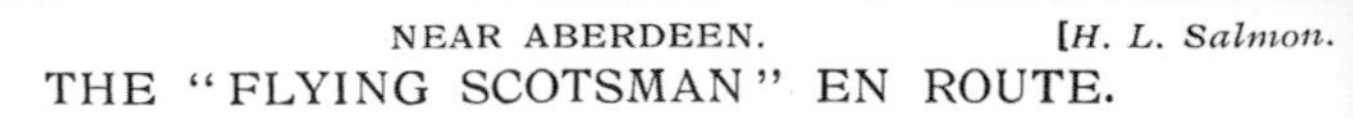

NEAR ABERDEEN. [*H. L. Salmon.*

THE "FLYING SCOTSMAN" EN ROUTE.

generally within view of the sea and with a distant glimpse of the Bell or Inchcape Rock and its famous lighthouse, but more particularly in a golfing world, seeing that golf links are laid out on each side of the line, apparently in endless succession, all the way from Monifieth to Carnoustie.

At Elliot Junction the Carmyllie Light Railway joins our route, and soon after we draw up at Arbroath, a busy and interesting manufacturing town. At St. Vigeans Junction we leave the Dundee and Arbroath Joint Line, and continue over another interesting section, with further views seawards, including the shores of Lunan Bay and the ruins of the old Red Castle of William the Lion. On this stage there are some steep stretches, particularly approaching Lunan Bay station, which involve gradients of 1 in 92 and 1 in 100 for north-bound trains, and 1 in 88 for south-bound.

As we near Montrose we enter upon a long single-track viaduct across the Harbour, so that we have water on each side. Rossie Island is about half-way across, dividing the two channels of the South Esk River.

After spending two or three minutes at Montrose, a linen, yarn and shipbuilding centre, the distinguishing feature of which is the tall spire of the parish church, we turn inland, leaving the Bervie branch to serve the coast for the time being. Again on single line, a steep climb carries us past Hillside, and almost immediately we start on a short stretch of 1 in 88 which takes us up to Kinnaber Junction—famous as the real winning post of the 1895 "Race to Aberdeen."

Dusk is falling, but there is still sufficient light to enable us to notice Dunnottar Castle on its precipitous cliff. As we continue on the "last lap" of our journey we can discern "Castle Rock," near Muchalls, and between Newtonhill and Portlethen we catch a glimpse of Findon Village—whence come the smoked haddocks generally known as "Finnan haddies"—as it nestles in one of the rocky coves which reveal themselves every now and then as we speed along.

Then down a long incline of seven miles through Cove our "Atlantic" gives us a final example of fast running, though we hope, during our stay in Aberdeen, to see some of the beauties of this stretch of coast under more leisured conditions, until at Ferryhill Junction we slow up for our last half-mile into Aberdeen's great station.

Entering the station we notice hurriedly some of the neat little engines of the Great North of Scotland section of the L.N.E.R. We are not, indeed, at the extreme point of a possible through East Coast Route journey. To do that would involve another 124 miles right up to Elgin and Lossiemouth. But we have come to the end of our journey by the "Flying Scotsman," and as it is 10.5 p.m., five minutes over 12 hours since we left King's Cross, we are well pleased to say good-bye to our reserved compartment, comfortable though it has been, and, with the assistance of a red-coated L.N.E.R.

Hotel Porter, wend our way along No. 6 platform to the private passage and lift leading directly into the Palace Hotel, where, accommodation having been previously booked, we find everything up to the best L.N.E.R. Hotel standard, and so to bed.

Next day we have an opportunity to look round the station—neat and spacious and well equipped in every way, seeing that the work of entire reconstruction was finished only about 10 years ago. L.N.E.R. trains work from both ends, southwards to the Deeside line which diverges at Ferryhill Junction, as well as to Dundee and Edinburgh, and northwards to Cruden Bay and Boddam, Fraserburgh and Peterhead, Banff and Macduff, Grantown-on-Spey and Boat of Garten, and via Craigellachie or via Buckie to Elgin, and thence to Inverness. There are 13 platforms, some terminal, but four are of double length and serve for the heavy East Coast expresses, and for the working of through trains or through coaches, such as the Elgin and Lossiemouth vehicles which are worked through in connection with certain Edinburgh-Aberdeen expresses, and, with a sleeping car, all the way from London on one of the night expresses.

The station ranks, indeed, as one of the largest and most notable in the British Isles, and it possesses certain features suggestive of Waverley, Edinburgh, in that it also is spanned by a great arch (carrying Union Street) over the line, while there is a lower bridge more centrally located, adjacent to which are the

THE "FLYING SCOTSMAN" LEAVING ABERDEEN FOR LONDON.

railway offices. A busy station, and one of continual interest, well adapted to meet the requirements of the "Granite City," whether regarded as an industrial and trading centre, as a great fishing port, or as a splendid tourist headquarters and a seaside resort. But that is another story, for which space is not available here, though a little more is told in Chapter XI.

Finally, before concluding this section, it is necessary to make a few remarks in reference to the up "Flying Scotsman." So far as Glasgow, Perth and Edinburgh are concerned, the 10 o'clock may have the same class of passengers as on the down journey, in that to leave Queen Street, Glasgow, at 8.40 a.m., and Perth at 8.30 a.m., is not inconveniently early in view of the fact that the train lands passengers in London at 6.15 the same evening. But 6.15 a.m. is not quite a time which tourist passengers would select to leave Aberdeen, and even Dundee at 8.9 a.m. is rather early, so that, although the up "Flying Scotsman" has an Aberdeen portion, as in the case of its down counterpart, the greater proportion of the passengers who travel by the 10 o'clock from King's Cross select instead the 9.50 a.m. from Aberdeen, connecting with the 1.15 p.m. train from Edinburgh, due in London at 10 p.m.

So far as the carriages are concerned, however, the up "Flying Scotsman" has the same sections as the down train, the Aberdeen part (with a Breakfast Car) coming in at 9.42 a.m., the Perth section at 9.50 a.m., and the Glasgow vehicles at 9.48 a.m. All these trains usually come in on the up side of Waverley station, and whether at the long up main platform or at one of the terminal lines at the west end, there is a busy ten minutes as the trains are split up and the through coaches shunted on to the waiting Edinburgh coaches. Indeed, at times when the 10 o'clock is run in two parts, it is more usual to combine the Aberdeen coaches only with the main Edinburgh train at 10 a.m., and to attach the Perth and Glasgow vehicles to the second part at 10.15 a.m. This averages the loading rather more equally, and gives a few minutes longer for the complicated shunting—a big advantage when traffic is as heavy as it is at Waverley station at holiday periods and during the summer.

Otherwise, the up train is generally worked more or less in the same way as the down "Flying Scotsman," except that Aberdeen passengers have Breakfast, Luncheon and Tea on the journey up, instead of Luncheon, Tea and Dinner, and the arrival in London is in the early evening instead of 10 o'clock. As, however, no tourist who has travelled right through to Aberdeen on the outward journey, as we did, can possibly afford to miss at least a day or two in Edinburgh, he will, no doubt, prefer to leave Aberdeen by the 9.50 a.m. (in company with the Aberdeen-Penzance through coaches), going on to London the next day or a day or so after by the Edinburgh "Flying Scotsman."

CHAPTER XI.

WHERE THE "FLYING SCOTSMAN" WILL TAKE YOU.

SO far, we have considered the "Flying Scotsman" mainly as an express connecting London with Edinburgh, Glasgow, Perth, Dundee and Aberdeen. In practice, however, it does a great deal more than that. For one thing, although when two trains are run the true "Flying Scotsman" is not usually available for passengers from London to Grantham, York and Newcastle, either the main train or its relief provides in one way or another for these journeys, as also for connections with other trains at these stations. Further, at the stations where it calls, to compensate for passengers who may leave, others join for the journey north, and even if the 10 o'clock were rigidly restricted to passengers for Edinburgh and beyond, there is a tremendous range of possible destinations west and north of the Scottish capital.

Consequently, while the "Flying Scotsman" is essentially an express for Edinburgh, that city is, for a large proportion of the passengers, merely the "Gateway to Scotland" as a whole. By changing at Berwick (for places in the south of Scotland), Waverley (Edinburgh), Glasgow, Dundee, Perth or Aberdeen, as well as any other Scottish station at which the main or connecting trains call, the passenger is given a convenient route to practically every part of Scotland.

Hence, we find at practically every principal or junction station in Scotland, at least one train, and sometimes several more, in connection, bringing passengers to join us, or distributing those who leave us. In one respect, only, is the range of service of the "Flying Scotsman" less than that of the night expresses of the East Coast Route, and that is in regard to journeys beyond Glasgow, Perth or Aberdeen, for the simple reason that, arriving in the late evening, no one requires to continue on for another 100 miles or so in order to reach a final destination during the early hours of the morning. Consequently, the through coaches for Elgin and Lossiemouth, Inverness and Fort William and Mallaig, are provided only on night trains, when sleeping cars are added.

But while the "Flying Scotsman" does not itself include through carriages for these destinations, it usually carries large numbers of passengers holding through tickets or taking advantage of the generous tourist tickets arranged by the London and North Eastern Railway. Sometimes the journey is broken at Edinburgh simply in order to make a break, but the majority do so with a view to exploring Edinburgh and taking advantage of the many touring facilities for which it is so splendid a centre. Indeed, for any visitor to Scotland to neglect its capital, unless from sheer

EDINBURGH.

DUNDEE. *[J. Valentine.*

ABERDEEN. [*Photochrom*

PERTH. [*Photochrom.*

necessity, would be to plead guilty to "wilful negligence" or the misuse of one's opportunities.

Glasgow, too, though "obtrusively industrial" in the main—yet no one ought to neglect seeing something of the commercial and manufacturing capital of Scotland—is a centre for tourist expeditions on a scale almost if not quite unsurpassed. Within easy reach, at small expense and with every convenience, is the Firth of Clyde, with its wonderful scenic attractions and steamer services in all directions, accessible via Craigendoran Pier (L.N.E.R.), or by steamer all the way from Glasgow's great landing stage, the Broomielaw. Some of the steamers go far afield, through the Kyles of Bute and the Crinan Canal, to the Western Islands, or round the coast to Oban, Fort William and to Inverness through the Caledonian Canal. Via Balloch, a bare hour's journey will take you to Loch Lomond and its 20 miles or so of mountain-encompassed and island-studded waters. One can also go still further, and in the course of a comfortable day's tour make the world-famous "Trossachs" trip, out to Balloch by rail, steamer on Loch Lomond to Rowardennan Pier, coach thence to Stronachlachar, steamer on Loch Katrine to Aberfoyle, and home by rail; or the tour may be made in the reverse order.

From Edinburgh one can also make the same tour with through coaches on the rail sections, while one can further explore the Scott country by means of the L.N.E.R. "Waverley" route. From Edinburgh, also, as well as from Glasgow, and with the advantage of through carriages, one can travel by day over the wonderful West Highland line to Fort William (for Ben Nevis and the steamers to Oban or Inverness via the Caledonian Canal), or through to Mallaig. The West Highland is, indeed, probably Britain's finest scenic line, one hundred miles of unsurpassed mountain, loch and river scenery, sometimes grand by reason of its very bareness and bleakness, at other times magnificent because of its wooded beauty.

Perth gives access to the attractions of the Grampians, the beauty of the Pass of Killiecrankie and the mountain splendours of the Dunkeld route to Inverness, the "Capital of the Highlands." It is true that, beyond Perth, we are no longer on the London and North Eastern Railway, but that company provides through vehicles and includes all required facilities, so that the passenger has the full value of the L.N.E.R. connections with the old Highland Railway, and due advantage of the fact that to Inverness as to Aberdeen, Dundee and Edinburgh, the L.N.E.R. provides the shortest route.

At Aberdeen the L.N.E.R. connects with its most northerly section, the late Great North of Scotland Railway, whose lines radiate in all directions west and north of Aberdeen. First there is the Deeside line, for Banchory and Ballater, and by railway motor omnibus or motor coach to Balmoral and Braemar, names which, in a sense, visualise their tourist and scenic

GLASGOW. [*Photochrom.*

L.N.E.R. STEAMER "TALISMAN," AT INNELLAN. [*C. J. L. Romanes.*

FORT WILLIAM. [*Photochrom.*

MALLAIG. [*Robinson.*

attractions. North there are the alternative main lines to Elgin and Lossiemouth, one via the chain of picturesque fishing ports on Moray Firth, the other via Craigellachie and beautiful Speyside. Both routes also give through facilities to Inverness, many tourists going that way either from choice or as an alternative to the Dunkeld route from Perth. There are also the branches to Banff and Macduff, Peterhead and Fraserburgh, Cruden Bay, Boddam, and the Alford Valley line, not to mention the picturesque Speyside line from Craigellachie to Grantown-on-Spey and Boat of Garten, all names which are synonymous with scenic beauty and tourist interest to the Southerner, as well as to the lowland Scotsman.

But while it is easy to mention all these attractions, it is, after all, the character and the cost of the railway arrangements which call for primary consideration, so far as the average tourist is concerned, and in this respect the London and North Eastern Railway provides an exceptionally generous range of facilities. Thus, practically all tourist tickets for Scotland allow of the use of three alternative routes south of York, and via Berwick or via Hexham and the "Waverley" route between Newcastle and Edinburgh. North of Edinburgh practically any possible route is available. One can travel to the Clyde resorts via Edinburgh, Glasgow and Craigendoran Pier. To the West Highland line, though it is possible to travel by through carriages in one stage by night trains, a better course is to spend a day at Edinburgh, and then proceed from Edinburgh by through coaches attached to the day trains via Glasgow, Craigendoran and Crianlarich. By utilising break of journey facilities, which apply at all principal and many intermediate stations, one can digress for special tours, such as the Trossachs, or a trip on Loch Lomond. One can, indeed, cover part of the West Highland route by utilising the Loch Lomond steamers from Balloch to Ardlui.

To Inverness one can travel either via Perth and Dunkeld or via Aberdeen and Elgin, or one way out and the other home, by booking appropriately, and there are many alternatives which do not require such forethought.

In this connection a great deal of variety can be introduced without incurring any additional expense over that for the direct journey, or at very small proportionate extra cost, as to which the tourist programmes issued by the L.N.E.R. are well worthy of careful study. A certain degree of apparent complexity is inevitable, owing to the wide range of facilities offered, but this complexity vanishes if the booklet is studied with the aid of a map, as included in many of the railway publications and in the time-tables.

There are also combined tourist tickets in association with McBrayne's and other steamers, providing for reaching Oban, Fort William or Inverness by utilising some of the popular steamer excursions operated in all directions on the Scottish lochs, and among the Hebrides. Another interesting feature

LOCH LOMOND.

LOCH LONG. [*Photochrom.*

is provided by the motor omnibus and motor coach services characteristic of the Great North of Scotland section, particularly the Deeside, Donside and Speyside " Three Rivers " and other tours.

Each and all of these are convenient additions to, and extensions of, the journey of the " Flying Scotsman," whether used to Edinburgh, Glasgow, Perth or Aberdeen. It is possible to travel more cheaply by the good, fast and comfortable excursion trains which are run by the L.N.E.R. at week-ends during the holiday months and at " Bank Holiday " periods, but unless cost is an essential factor the tourist will be well advised to travel " tourist," and thus get the advantage of the alternative route and break of journey facilities then available. Incidentally, and in order to appreciate the scenic attractions of the East Coast Route to the full, he will have the opportunity and privilege of travelling by the world's most famous and oldest-established express train, with its most up-to-date accommodation and restaurant car equipment, the " Flying Scotsman."

LONDON & NORTH EASTERN RAILWAY

INTERESTING PUBLICATIONS

DEALING WITH THE

"FLYING SCOTSMAN" LOCOMOTIVE,

ETC.

PHOTOGRAPH OF "FLYING SCOTSMAN":—

Actual photograph of the "Pacific" engine, "Flying Scotsman," exhibited at the British Empire Exhibition, with interesting dimensions. Size 11 ins. by 7 ins. *Price 1s., post free.*

POSTCARD OF "FLYING SCOTSMAN" ENGINE IN COLOURS. *Price 1d., by post 1½d.*

POSTCARD OF "LOCOMOTION NO. 1" (1825) IN COLOURS.
Price 1d., by post 1½d.

COLOURED PLATE OF "FLYING SCOTSMAN."

Coloured Plate 25 ins. by 11 ins. of "Flying Scotsman" Engine. *Price 1s. 6d., post free.*

CARDBOARD MODELS OF LOCOMOTIVES:—

Scale models of "Locomotion No. 1" (1825), and "Flying Scotsman," the first and latest type passenger engines, with instructions for cutting out and assembling. *Price 6d. per set, by post 8d.*

CARDBOARD MODELS OF CARRIAGES:—

Scale models of the old "Experiment" Coach (1825) and latest sleeping carriage, with instructions for cutting out and assembling. *Price 6d. per set, by post 8d.*

"THE RAILWAY CENTENARY."

A book describing a century of railway development. *Price 3s. 6d.*

RAILWAY CENTENARY POSTCARDS:—

Postcard views of old and modern engines and trains, and public notices of 100 years ago. *Price 1s. 6d. per packet of 12 cards, post free.*

These publications are obtainable from L.N.E.R. Offices and Stations, or from the Advertising Manager, 26, Pancras Road, London, N.W.1.; York; or Waverley Station, Edinburgh.